Florida's People During the Last Ice Age

Florida A&M University, Tallahassee
Florida Atlantic University, Boca Raton
Florida Gulf Coast University, Ft. Myers
Florida International University, Miami
Florida State University, Tallahassee
New College of Florida, Sarasota
University of Central Florida, Orlando
University of Florida, Gainesville
University of North Florida, Jacksonville
University of South Florida, Tampa
University of West Florida, Pensacola

FLORIDA'S PEOPLE DURING THE LAST ICE AGE

Barbara A. Purdy

Foreword by James S. Dunbar

University Press of Florida

Gainesville · Tallahassee · Tampa · Boca Raton

Pensacola · Orlando · Miami · Jacksonville · Ft. Myers · Sarasota

Copyright 2008 by Barbara A. Purdy
Printed in the United States of America on acid-free paper
All rights reserved

13 12 11 10 09 08   6 5 4 3 2 1

Library of Congress Cataloging-in-Publication Data
Purdy, Barbara A.
Florida's people during the last ice age / Barbara A. Purdy ; foreword by James S. Dunbar.
p. cm.
Includes bibliographical references and index.
ISBN 978-0-8130-3204-7 (alk. paper)
1. Paleo-Indians—Florida. 2. Excavations (Archaeology)—Florida. 3. Florida—
Antiquities. I. Title.
E78.F6P86 2008
975.9'01—dc22   2007027536

The University Press of Florida is the scholarly publishing agency for the State University
System of Florida, comprising Florida A&M University, Florida Atlantic University,
Florida Gulf Coast University, Florida International University, Florida State University,
New College of Florida, University of Central Florida, University of Florida, University
of North Florida, University of South Florida, and University of West Florida.

University Press of Florida
15 Northwest 15th Street
Gainesville, FL 32611-2079
http://www.upf.com

To E. H. Sellards, a man of vision

In January 1565, René Laudonnière, the governor of Fort Caroline, a French Huguenot colony located near the mouth of the St. Johns River, feigned friendship as he interrogated two Spaniards who had for many years been prisoners of Indians living south of present-day Cape Canaveral. Laudonnière's eye fell upon a pendant one of the Spaniards wore around his neck.

"What a curious ornament. It looks like a horse tooth."

"A very old, old horse, I think," said the Spaniard. "Near the Atlantic coast, in the land of the Ais, there are layers of earth that contain all manner of bones from strange creatures, including elephants and tigers. The tooth came from the same layer."

This is the earliest reference to Florida's extensive deposits of extinct fossil animals.

Contents

Figures

Foreword

They say timing is everything, and with this book Barbara Purdy has impeccable timing. Publication of *Florida's People During the Last Ice Age* coincides with the centennial celebration of the Florida Geological Survey (FGS), honoring individuals such as E. H. Sellards, for placing prehistoric peoples side by side with Pleistocene megafauna. In 1904, E. H. Sellards began his career as a professor of geology and zoology at the University of Florida. In 1907. he accepted the job as Florida's first state geologist. He and his staff almost immediately began reporting spectacular finds of fossilized mega-mammal bones and prehistoric artifacts. Nowhere were any of the discoveries as sensational as at the Vero Man site in Brevard County. Sellards, conducting excavations at Vero, and Frederic B. Loomis and James W. Gidley, conducting investigations at the neighboring Melbourne Man site, found human remains, artifacts, and fossil mega-mammal bones in stratigraphic association. If correct, they were destined to be the first researchers to demonstrate that prehistoric people coexisted with now extinct mega-mammals such as the mastodon and mammoth. Instead, they found controversy and became embroiled in academic arguments with Rollin T. Chamberlin and Aleš Hrdlička about the integrity of their finds. The controversy at the Vero and Melbourne sites was never settled, so the question remained: Did people live in the New World during the Pleistocene?

In 1918, Sellards moved to Austin to take a job at the University of Texas, Bureau of Economic Geology. He continued research on Pleistocene sites with human artifacts, and, before retiring, he published the acclaimed work *Early Man in America* (1952). This book documented what had already become accepted by archaeologists: Paleoindians occupied North America during the Pleistocene and hunted now extinct mega-mammals, including mammoths. The scholar who began his career in

Florida was among those who set the scientific record straight, and it is timely that Dr. Purdy has detailed the Florida "chapter" of his story.

The focus of Dr. Purdy's book is not intended to solve the never-ending thirst for knowledge and the tensions among scientists as they attempt to seek truth. The book is intended to provide historical understanding of the changing contexts of the research and researchers and some of the progress that has been made in the discipline. In this regard, she has done an especially admirable job.

One of Florida's most published archaeologists, Barbara Purdy leads us through the colorful, although now and then painful, episodes of discovery and research on Paleoindian sites in Florida. Beginning with some of the earliest incidental discoveries and ending with some of the latest research, she provides insight into some of the little-known, established, and high-profile site investigations and their investigators. She discusses the characters, the speculators, the researchers and their contributions and controversies. It is a welcome summary of what has gone before and gives some sense of what might take place tomorrow. This is both a good source and overview for interested avocationals and professionals alike.

James S. Dunbar

Preface

It is hard to imagine that Florida was affected by the Ice Ages. Glaciers certainly did not come this far south, and the landscape was not scoured by their advances and retreats as occurred in other areas. Growing ice masses, however, lowered worldwide sea levels by 300 feet (100 meters) and captured Florida's water supply. If a present-day map of the state were compared to a hypothesized version 12,000–18,000 years old, one would notice that rivers disappear, lake basins are empty, and the coastline extends far beyond its current borders. Fresh water would be difficult to find and procure, available only in much-reduced springs and sinkholes that enticed people and animals to risk their lives for this necessary resource. The vegetation also would not resemble that of today and has been compared to a desert or an African savannah. Lake basins began to fill about 8,000 years ago, and widespread, more or less modern climatic and environmental conditions emerged around 5,000–6,000 years ago. By that time, Late Pleistocene megafauna were long extinct.

While many books mention Florida's people and animals during the last Ice Age as a segment of a broader discussion of the state's prehistoric and early historic cultures, this book is the first effort to focus solely on this fascinating topic. It was a longer journey than I anticipated, and if you bear with me throughout the following pages, you will conclude, as I have done, that the journey has not ended. The task of identifying the mysterious first Floridians and their prey is not easy, but the good news is that twenty-first-century technology might make the job achievable.

Acknowledgments

My interest in the peopling of the Western Hemisphere dates to the 1960s when I lived in the state of Washington and worked with Dr. Richard D. Daugherty, who excavated famous ancient sites such as Lind Coulee and Marmes Rockshelter. Thanks, Dick.

I will list in alphabetical order the assistance of the many people who helped me obtain documents, pictures, objects, and permissions for this volume from the Florida Museum of Natural History, Special Collections of the University of Florida Library, Silver River Museum, Silver Springs, Florida Geological Survey, Florida Bureau of Archaeological Research, Florida State University, Rosenstiel School of Marine and Atmospheric Science at the University of Miami, Southeastern Archaeological Research, Inc., Bland & Associates, Inc., National Museum of Natural History, Amherst College, Barnard College of Columbia University, New York University, and additional sources: David Anderson, Susan Anton, Robert Austin, Myles C.P. Bland, Ann Cordell, James Cusick, James S. Dunbar, Jeff Gage, John A. Gifford, C. Andrew Hemmings, Alvin Hendrix, Richard Hulbert, James Krakker, Elise V. LeCompte, Guy Marwick, Guy H. Means, Scott Mitchell, Nan A. Rothschild, Donna Ruhl, Thomas M. Scott, Steve Specht, Laura Taylor, Louis D. Tesar, Gwen Thompson, David Thulman, S. David Webb, and Debra J. Wells.

Thanks also to Albert C. Goodyear, Robert L. Knight, David Leigh, Jeffrey M. Mitchem, Jim O'Sullivan, Tom Pertierra, Thomas W. Stafford Jr., Sam Upchurch, and William J. Whitehurst for their stimulating comments and cooperation.

Special thanks to Laura Taylor, who, as a student at Amherst College in Massachusetts, found documents and pictures from Professor Frederick Loomis's 1923 investigations at Melbourne, Florida.

The comments and suggestions from the two reviewers were invaluable. Any remaining errors are mine alone.

And finally, a huge thank-you to Laurence H. Purdy for not only helping with many logistics associated with this book but also for putting up with me during its preparation.

Introduction

Florida is one of the most fascinating places on earth. Did you know that

- Between 550 and 250 million years ago, Florida was not part of North America and was located 50° south of the equator?
- No dinosaur bones have ever been found in Florida even though dinosaurs roamed the continent from 250 million years ago until they became extinct around 65 million years ago? Florida was underwater most of the time from about 65 million years ago until 15–20 million years ago, and any dinosaur remains that might be preserved are buried beneath thousands of feet of limestone deposits.
- The oldest rocks exposed on the surface in Florida are only 42–44 million years old and represent a mere 1 percent of earth's geologic history?
- Little would be known about the terrestrial vertebrates in eastern North America from about 33 million years ago until 4 million years ago if it weren't for Florida's rich fossil record? Some of these animals, including the giant ground sloth, camel, horse, tapir, elephant, rhinoceros, and saber-toothed tiger, eventually became extinct in this part of the world thousands or tens of thousands of years ago. The horse returned with the Spanish in the 1500s.
- The earth's climate began to cool occasionally around 30 million years ago and glaciers formed in Antarctica, but the time period known as the Ice Ages or Pleistocene Epoch is less than 2.5 million years old?

For more interesting facts and greater details about Florida's ancient geology, paleontology, and climate, see Randazzo and Jones (1997), Hulbert (2001), and their references.

The last Ice Age (fourth major glacial advance) began more than 50,000 years ago. The environmental history of Florida during the latter part of the last Ice Age (approximately 30,000 to 13,000 years ago) is as exciting as the events mentioned above, especially after the species *Homo sapiens* appeared on the scene. And that is what this book is all about.

Setting the Stage

The time and place of the arrival of humans in the Western Hemisphere and their spread throughout the Americas has been a fiercely debated issue for several hundred years and still is not resolved. In this volume, I will focus on this problem as it relates to Florida. My objectives are to

- Discuss obstacles that have prohibited archaeologists from proving or refuting claims of great antiquity for humans in Florida and elsewhere in the Western Hemisphere.
- Examine the indisputable evidence documenting the earliest human presence in Florida, which at this time is about 14,000 years ago.
- Examine evidence that suggests people were in Florida earlier than 14,000 years ago.
- Recommend twenty-first-century technology and expertise that could be utilized to shed light on this enduring mystery.
- Separate fact from fantasy, proof from spoof.

Background

When Christopher Columbus and those who followed him came in contact with Native Americans, they wondered where these people originated. Their presence had to be explained because, according to Judeo-Christian teachings, all human beings are descended from Adam and Eve, the first man and woman created by God in the Old World. Interestingly, as early as 1589, José de Acosta, a Jesuit friar, suggested that the Indians came from Asia "by shipwracke or tempest of whether," or across a land bridge far to the north. This amazing hypothesis by the learned priest was advanced prior to any known exploration in the area. Subsequently, James Adair (1775) and many other early scholars proposed a Jewish origin for the American aborigines. They believed that the Indians derived from the Lost Tribes of Israel and that they had passed across the Bering Strait and made their way southward. According to Swanton (1946: 22), the traditions of most tribes, at least in the southeastern United States, indicate a belief that they came from the northwest. Since there are well-documented records of shifting settlements after the contact period, many of these stories could refer to the recent past rather than ancient lore.

Creation myths and migration legends were passed down orally generation after generation by preliterate peoples throughout the world. They became embellished and distorted through time, making it difficult to separate truth from fantasy. From 1492 to the twentieth century, the origin tales of the New World aborigines were set down in writing by missionaries and other newcomers to the Americas. Many were not recorded until long after the contact period, and it is impossible to determine how profoundly they were influenced by the religious beliefs of European Christians. Stories varied from group to group and were modified to fit specific circumstances and geographic areas. Here is an example of a Cherokee creation myth:

Long ago, before there were any people, the world was young and water covered everything. The earth was a great island floating above the seas, suspended by four rawhide ropes representing the four sacred directions. It hung down from the crystal sky. There were no people, but the animals lived in a home above the rainbow. Needing space, they sent Water Beetle to search for room under the seas. Water Beetle dove deep and brought up mud that spread quickly, turning into land that was flat and too soft and wet for the animals to live on.

Grandfather Buzzard was sent to see if the land had hardened. When he flew over the earth, he found the mud had become solid;

he flapped in for a closer look. The wind from his wings created valleys and mountains.

As the land stiffened, the animals came down from the rainbow. It was still dark. They needed light, so they pulled the sun out from behind the rainbow, but it was too bright and hot. A solution was urgently needed. The shamans were told to place the sun higher in the sky. A path was made for it to travel—from east to west—so that all inhabitants could share in the light.

The plants were placed upon the earth. The Creator told the plants and animals to stay awake for seven days and seven nights. Only a few animals managed to do so, including the owls and mountain lions, and they were rewarded with the power to see in the dark. Among the plants, only the cedars, spruces, and pines remained awake. The Creator told these plants that they would keep their hair during the winter, while the other plants would lose theirs.

People were created last. The women were able to have babies every seven days. They reproduced so quickly that the Creator feared the world would soon become too crowded. So after that the women could have only one child per year, and it has been that way ever since. (from Andrews 2006)

Speculations and creation myths are intriguing, but the factual answer to the question of human origins in the Americas must depend upon research by archaeologists and their colleagues from geology, paleontology, paleobotany, climatology, soils, physical anthropology, archaeometry, and other contributing scientific fields. There is no other way. As eloquently stated by a distinguished archaeologist, the late Dr. Jesse D. Jennings, "The story I tell is of the American Indian before the writing of history began. It is a story no scribe ever carved in stone, no wise old chieftain ever told to a circle of eager young faces. Archaeologists have had to tease it from the stubborn earth at a thousand places where its paragraphs and chapters lay hidden beneath the sediment of ages" (Jennings 1974:29).

1

Reports of Possible Ice Age Human Presence in Florida, 1850–1950

In the seventeenth century, Archbishop James Ussher calculated that God created the world on October 23, 4004 B.C. Ussher's chronology allowed only 6,000 years for all human history (there was no prehistory). Although discoveries of artifacts in association with extinct animals were reported previously, his theory became theological dogma that was not disproved indisputably until 1859. Jacques Boucher de Perthes had been collecting stone tools and extinct animal bones from sealed gravels of the Somme River in northern France since 1837. De Perthes was ridiculed by the scientific community when he claimed that the stone tools and animals existed before the biblical flood. Eventually, however, his sites were examined by two leading British scholars who verified that his finds were evidence of long antiquity for humankind. About the same time, quarry workers in the Neander Valley, Germany, unearthed a primitive-looking skull. This and similar specimens have since been known as "Neanderthals" (Fig. 1.1). Prehistory (a past before written records) was born as the theories of uniformitarianism and evolution, advanced by Charles Darwin and Thomas Huxley, were gradually accepted (Fagan 1991: 39–42; Renfrew and Bahn 1991: 22).

Thus it was during the late nineteenth and early twentieth centuries, soon after the presence of pre-modern people (Neantherthals) was confirmed in Europe, that discoveries of ancient humans in the Americas were reported by farmers, construction workers, and hoaxers. Hrdlička (1907, 1918) and others (e.g., Holmes 1919: xiii, 104) attempted to evaluate objectively stories of "glacial man" from California, Michigan, New Jersey, Nebraska, and elsewhere. In most cases, they correctly dismissed claims of great antiquity by careful scrutiny of the evidence, but they could not

Fig. 1.1. A nineteenth-century conception of a Neanderthal individual.

always explain how human remains became incorporated into glacial strata or why they were associated with extinct fauna. When either occurred, they concluded that "we may wisely await the results of further research and provide for the application to these of the severest tests that science can devise" (Holmes 1919: 94). Basically, Hrdlička, Holmes, and their colleagues were reacting against sensationalism and unfounded presumptions about the presence of primitive forms of the species *Homo sapiens* in the Western Hemisphere. When the opportunity arose for them to examine specimens themselves, they stressed the fact that the bones looked no different than those of present-day Indian populations and, therefore, could not date to the Pleistocene. It is within the context of this state of affairs that the following Florida cases were judged (Fig. 1.2).

Lake Monroe

"These remains cannot properly be said to belong to the shell heap, as they are in the sandstone underlying it. The burial was no doubt older than the shell heap" (Wyman 1875: 18–19). Wyman is referring to Stone Island (aka Rock Island or Doctor's Island) on the north shore of Lake Monroe, Volusia County, where, in 1848, Count L. F. de Pourtalés discovered a human jaw with perfect teeth and other bones embedded in freshwater sandstone. Unfortunately, various accounts of the discovery erroneously stated that the bones came from an ancient coral reef (marine deposit) instead of freshwater sandstone. According to Wyman (1875), Count

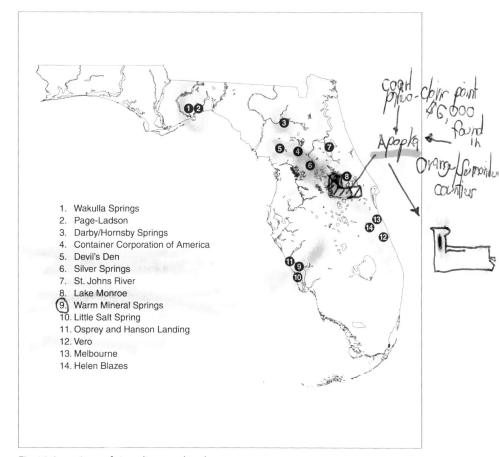

1. Wakulla Springs
2. Page-Ladson
3. Darby/Hornsby Springs
4. Container Corporation of America
5. Devil's Den
6. Silver Springs
7. St. Johns River
8. Lake Monroe
9. Warm Mineral Springs
10. Little Salt Spring
11. Osprey and Hanson Landing
12. Vero
13. Melbourne
14. Helen Blazes

Fig. 1.2. Locations of sites discussed in the text.

Pourtalés attempted to correct this mistake, but the misconception was perpetuated by such famous people as Louis Agassiz (in Nott and Gliddon 1854: 352), Sir Charles Lyell (1863: 44–45), and Aleš Hrdlička (1907: 19). In 1874, Wyman also found portions of a human skeleton in the sandstone and concluded they were part of the same individual: "The bones have lost their organic matter, and, where broken, show that all cavities are filled with fine sand, which has become consolidated with the bony tissue" (Wyman 1875: 19). From the sandstone, he recovered bones of deer, alligator, and soft-shell turtle, but no extinct species were reported. Neither he nor the Count recorded the depth or precise location of the human remains, and it is not known if they are in storage somewhere today awaiting further study.

Beginning in 1987 and continuing off and on until 1993, I directed archaeological investigations in waterlogged deposits of a large Indian shell mound on the north shore of Lake Monroe, a short distance west of Stone Island. Nearly 2 meters below surface, at the contact of the shell midden with underlying sand (not cemented), hickory nut fragments returned dates of 6200 RCYBP (radiocarbon years before present). If calibrated (see Dating), the hickory nuts would be about 7000–8000 calendar years old (Purdy 2001: 38–47). It is possible that the skeleton found in 1848 by Count Pourtalés is at least this age or much older.

Osprey and Hanson Landing

Between 1871 and 1888, fossilized human bones were reported from several places along the Gulf Coast about twelve miles south of Sarasota. These locations were at Osprey, North Osprey, Hanson Landing, and South Osprey (Fig. 1.3).

The Osprey skull was discovered when a local landowner, J. G. Webb, was ditching in a hammock adjacent to his home, which was situated on a shell midden. Webb clearly understood the difference between a shell midden burial and the one he found: "It was intentionally buried . . . but had become surrounded by a soft, ferruginous rock, which is constantly forming wherever a spring comes to the surface" (letter to Professor Joseph Henry, June 4, 1871). The skull was sent to the Smithsonian Institu-

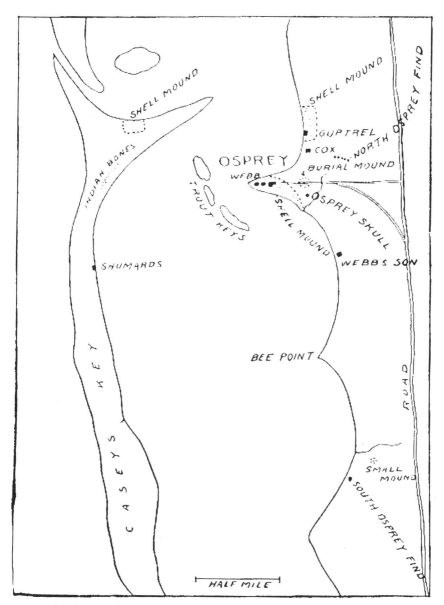

Fig. 1.3. Sketch map of Osprey and vicinity (Hrdlička 1907: 54).

tion (and may still be there), where it was concluded that it belonged to either a subadult or a small adult male, that it exhibited no deformity or disease, and that "anatomical indications of great antiquity are wholly lacking" (Hrdlička 1907: 58; Leidy 1889: 11–12). Leidy said that "the skull aproximates in shape an ordinary prepared French skull," and Hrdlička concluded, "it is safe to say that from the somatological standpoint there is absolutely nothing about the specimen which could not be found in recent crania of Florida Indians" (Hrdlička 1907: Plate VIa). Later, other bones presumably of the same individual were found but never studied.

In 1872, Webb and his son recovered human bones at North Osprey about a ten-minute walk from the first discovery. These remains were fossilized but of a different nature from that of the Osprey skull. There were about twenty bones including pieces of two male skulls with worn-down teeth. Again, Hrdlička (1907: 58–59) reports that there is nothing unusual about the skeletons to suggest great antiquity. The bones were sent to the Smithsonian, but a few pieces went to the Peabody Museum in Cambridge and still others to the Army Medical Museum.

About a discovery eight miles north of Osprey at Hanson Landing in 1886, Professor Angelo Heilprin wrote, "I was much surprised to find actually embedded in this [ferruginous] rock and more or less firmly united with it the skeletal remains of a mammalian which I had little difficulty in determining to be the genius Homo. . . . The distinctive cancellated stucture of bone is still plainly visible, but the bone itself has been completely replaced by limonite" (Heilprin 1887: 14–15). The remains seemed to belong to one individual and did not differ from recent humans. Some of the bones went to the University of Pennsylvania.

Along an eroding shore of Sarasota Bay, about a mile and a half south of Osprey in 1888, J. G. Webb and his son-in-law discovered a human skeleton embedded in and partly projecting from a conglomerate of red and black colored ferruginous rock (bog iron). In a letter to W. H. Dall, dated October 29, 1890, Webb says, "The mainland shores of the bay are wearing away very rapidly. The rock in which this specimen is embedded was not long ago covered by the soil and subsoil, which has been washed away." Two pieces of the rock in which the human bones occurred were chiseled out and sent to the Smithsonian Institution (see Hrdlička 1907:

Plate VIII). Hrdlička concluded that the bones, mostly vertebrae and ribs, all belonged to a single individual, apparently a male who was intentionally buried, and showed no unusual features.

In 1906, Hrdlička visited the Osprey localities accompanied by Dr. T. Wayland Vaughan, a geologist familiar with Florida formations. J. G. Webb, still in good health, guided them. At the original site, a trench was dug, 15 feet long, 6 feet wide, and no more than 3 feet deep. Although no additional bones were found, Hrdlička was able to see for himself the exact nature of the deposits in which human remains were recovered in 1871: 6 to 8 inches of black soil was underlain by white sand; at about 2 feet below surface the sand contained yellowish to rusty discoloration due to iron deposition; at 29 inches below surface and extending to the base of the excavation, a greenish layer was encountered consisting of sand, clay, and fine gravel of unknown thickness. The skull was found in the yellowish sandy layer (Fig. 1.4).

From his visit to the South Osprey location, Hrdlička noted that the shore continued to suffer from erosion as first described by Webb nearly twenty years earlier. Because of the mineralization of the water in the area, the conglomerate of ferruginous rock was forming continuously and

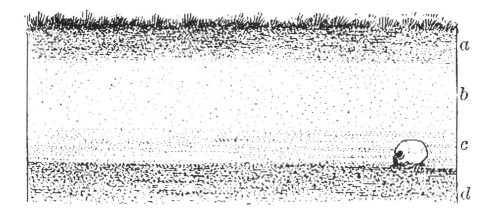

Fig. 1.4. Section of deposits showing position of the Osprey skull: (a) black soil mixed with sand, 15– 20 centimeters (6–8 inches); (b) white sand, showing yellow patches in lower parts due to ferringinous deposits, 50–60 centimeters (20–24 inches); (c) about where Osprey skull lay; (d) greenish clayey, sandy, and gravelly layer at 74 centimeters (29 inches) below surface, extent unknown (Hrdlička 1907: 61).

turning the sand and whatever it contained into cement. Webb and others had recovered pieces of Indian pottery, ancient cetaceans (marine mammals), sharks' teeth, and shells from a similar type of conglomerate in places along the shore.

Vaughan examined the geology of the Hanson Landing site and concluded that the ferruginous material there was similar to that at South Osprey: "It underlies surface soil and sand, consists of sand bound together by the brown oxide of iron, and occurs noncontinuously just above the water's edge. Therefore, I am of the opinion that the Hanson skull occurs in a geologically recent formation" (Vaughan 1907: 64–66).

Everyone involved in the Osprey and Hanson Landing sites attempted to evaluate the evidence objectively. They were all professional people. J. G. Webb was a judge and a learned individual, based on his letters to the Smithsonian. He described his discoveries accurately and did not sensationalize the situation. The main issue at the sites was the question of the antiquity of the human remains. They were embedded in ferruginous rock and were not part of local shell middens, although there were many shell middens in the area. Hrdlička feared, because of their unusual occurrence, that people would assume the bones belonged to pre-modern humans. This concern would not be an issue today. From the vantage point of more than 100 years of additional accumulated knowledge since the late nineteenth century, the overwhelming majority of present-day archaeologists would agree with Hrdlička that pre-modern humans never made it to the Western Hemisphere. However, artifacts, extinct animals, and skeletons of modern humans have now been found together at a few sites.

Unfortunately, as far as is known, no animal species or tools were associated with the burials at Osprey and Hanson Landing, but this situation could be a result of the retrieval methods utilized. Radiocarbon dating was not available at the time, but it would have been of little use because the skeletal remains are fossilized. It would be interesting to know how a geoarchaeologist and other specialists would investigate the finds and interpret the data today. Their objective conclusions might be vastly different from those of earlier scholars. There is probably no opportunity to restudy the sites, but maybe some of the human bones are still available for examination.

Central Atlantic Coast

Vero (8IR9)

The Indian River is more than 100 miles long and is separated from the Atlantic Ocean by a low barrier beach that rarely exceeds an elevation of 12 feet. Less than 15 miles from the ocean are the headwaters of the St. Johns River. The area between the Indian River and the St. Johns is occupied by flat, poorly drained prairies and forests (Fig. 1.5).

Vero (now Vero Beach) is located on the Atlantic Coast of central Florida. In November 1913, the Indian River Farms Company constructed a drainage canal that extended from the Indian River to about 13 miles in-

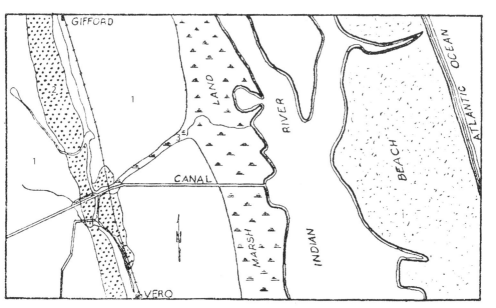

Fig. 1.5. Sketch map showing the locality near Vero where fossil human remains were found: (1) pine land; (2) sand dune; (3) stream valley. The human remains were found in the canal bank in this valley, west of the railroad (Sellards in MacCurdy 1937: 194).

land. Along the canal, especially where it intersected and drained an old streambed (Van Valkenburg Creek) and its north and south tributaries, vertebrate fossils were recovered by Isaac M. Weills and Frank Ayers in the bank and in sediments thrown out by the dredge (Fig. 1.6). Weills wrote to Dr. E. H. Sellards, the state geologist of Florida, and sent him some of the bones. Sellards realized the bones were well-preserved Pleistocene fossils. He visited the site and identified mammals, birds, batrachians, reptiles, and fishes. A few of the small mammals "have persisted to the present time, while the larger animals, including the elephants, mastodons, camels, horses, bison, tapirs, and sloths have suffered extinction" (Sellards 1916a: 123). Sellards suggested that Weills and Ayers keep a close watch for associated human remains in the bed containing the Pleistocene vertebrates (Sellards 1916a: 130, 1916b: 615). What prompted him to make this suggestion? Perhaps it resulted from the astounding announcement from England in 1912 that the "missing link" had been found. Piltdown Man had the head of a modern human with the jaw of an ape. This hoax was not exposed until the 1950s, when it was learned that the jaw of an orangutan, dead for 500 years, had been attached to the skull of a present-day human.

A more likely scenario follows. On February 5, 1914, newspapers throughout the United States "gave wide publicity to the retrieval of human bones in an asphalt pit at Rancho La Brea" in Los Angeles, California (Merriam 1914; Hrdlička 1918: 17). Rancho La Brea was already known for its valuable deposits of skeletal remains of Quaternary (Ice Age) fauna. It is quite probable that Sellards, because of his interests in similar fauna, was informed of this discovery and considered the possibility that a comparable situation might exist in Florida. In October 1915 and again in February, April, and June 1916, human bones were recovered with extinct Late Ice Age animals at Vero (Fig. 1.7). Their contemporaneity remains a debated issue to this day. In the following paragraphs, I describe the deposits and their contents as exposed by the canal construction and attempt to explain why there were believers and nonbelievers among professional colleagues who visited the site in October 1916, all of whom attempted to study the site in an unbiased manner (Sellards et al. 1917). Later, I will reexamine the evidence in light of more recent discoveries.

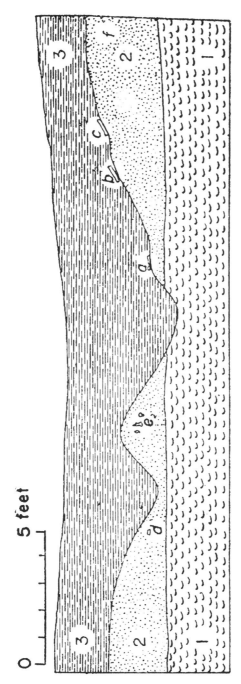

Fig. 1.6. Original face of Locality 2, Vero site, from 452 to 480 feet west of the railroad bridge. The numbers refer to the strata discussed in the text, and the letters refer to the human and artifactual remains (Rouse 1951:179, after Sellards 1916a: 137).

Fig. 1.7. The south bank where Vero skeletons 1 and 2 were found (see arrows). Taken from the highest elevation on the opposite bank of the canal (Hrdlička 1918: Plate I).

Sellards identified three major desposits at Vero:

- Stratum 1 (lowest) is the Anastasia Formation of marine shell and sand, which contained no vertebrates. Sellards named the formation in 1912 because the "shell marl was first quarried and described on Anastasia Island near St. Augustine, where it is known as Coquina" (Sellards 1912:18). The formation extends 200–300 miles along the East Coast.
- Stratum 2 (middle), subsequently called the Melbourne Formation (Cooke and Mossom 1929), is a freshwater deposit of rather coarse and fine sands containing vertebrates, land and freshwater invertebrates, plant fossils, human remains, and artifacts. "As a rule, the sand near the base of this stratum is light-colored and distinctly cross-bedded. . . . From 2 to 3 feet above the base of the stratum the sand loses its cross-bedding and becomes dark in color [and somewhat indurated], owing to the inclusion of organic matter" (Sellards et al. 1917: 8).

- Stratum 3 (top), subsequently named the Van Valkenburg Formation, consists chiefly of alternating layers of muck and light-colored sand containing vertebrates, land and freshwater invertebrates, plant fossils, human remains, and artifacts.

Each of the strata varied in thickness, averaging between 2 and 4 feet, but the average was greatly exceeded in some places and virtually nonexistent in others, especially in stratum 2.

There was general agreement that (1) the Anastasia Formation is a marine deposit and it graded into the freshwater sediments of stratum 2 and (2) the animals and plants of stratum 2 were Pleistocene in age. Disagreement arose about the human remains and artifacts that were found with the extinct fauna of stratum 2 and the base of stratum 3. Three reasons might be advanced to account for the controversy: (1) Hrdlička's belief that if human remains were in primary association with extinct animals, they should be a pre-modern physical type; (2) Oliver P. Hay's assertion that the vertebrate fauna in stratum 2 dated to the Early to Middle Pleistocene instead of (as we now know) the Late Pleistocene; and (3) Sellard's apparent failure to recognize initially that the boundary between strata 2 and 3, now called Melbourne/Van Valkenburg, represented an erosional zone of unknown duration and may have been an old sod line.

Sellards (1916a:127) suggested that stratum 2 was spring-fed and provided a freshwater resort for Pleistocene vertebrates. Thousands of animal bones and bone fragments were recovered in stratum 2 and the bottom of stratum 3. The broken bones may have resulted from trampling by succeeding generations of elephants or other large animals. Of the 49 species of animals identified, 28 are now extinct and only 14 species of the remainder still live in the vicinity. Plant remains did not survive in stratum 2 except for a few stems, acorn cups, and pieces of wood, which shriveled and fell apart when exposed to the air. However, marsh or swamp vegetation must have existed to satisfy the appetites of the multitude of animals that lived there. In addition, the bones would not have survived if they had not been entombed in a wet environment. Berry (1917: 19–33) studied the flora from stratum 3. Of the 27 species described, 19 are recent and 8 are found in Pliocene or Pleistocene deposits. Twenty of the species still grow at or near Vero (within 50 miles), 6 no longer occur in Peninsular Florida, and 1 of these is extinct. Berry concluded that the "flora is unquestionably of late Pleistocene age" and "indicates a more mesophytic habitat than exists today in the vicinity of Vero" (Berry 1917: 31–32).

Parts of two human skeletons were found in the south bank of the newly constructed canal. Skeleton I came from stratum 2 and Skeleton II from the contact of strata 2 and 3. A few smaller bones were recovered from the upper surface of stratum 2 and were thought to belong to Skeleton II. Three other individuals were represented by a shovel-shaped incisor of a juvenile or young adult, the upper molar of a young child, and a toe bone of an adult. Hrdlička (in Sellards et al. 1917: 43–51; Hrdlička 1918: 23–67) examined the situation surrounding the recovery of the bones, described the bones, and rendered his opinion of how the human elements managed to come to rest in deposits with Ice Age animals.

Skeleton I consisted of 23 bones, most of which were from the lower legs and feet and a lesser number from the left arm and both hands. Hrdlička (1918: 51) concluded that the skeleton was an adult woman, approximately 4 feet, 9 inches tall, and "plainly that of an individual possessing the essential osteological characteristics of the Florida and Eastern Indians; . . . it cannot possibly be classified as anything else than a skeleton of an ordinary Indian" (1918: 54).

Skeleton II (known as "Vero Man") consisted of 44 bones, including 16 pieces of skull, part of the lower jaw, a tooth, right scapula, 6 pieces of ribs, portions of the pelvis, left and right upper limbs, and left and right lower limbs. Hrdlička determined that Skeleton II was a male and somewhat advanced in life. "The individual was of tall stature, possibly not less than 5 feet, 10 inches, robust, and normal" (Hrdlička 1918: 56). Interestingly, he concluded, "the skull of Skeleton II by its lack of thickness, good size, and subdued supraorbital ridges is actually of a type superior to that of a large majority of the Florida Indians" (in Sellards et al. 1917: 50). And again, Hrdlička (1918: 55) says, "The skull and bones are Indian, but they seem to belong to a type such as can occasionally be found among the Eastern Algonquian, or among the Sioux, rather than in Florida. At first it seemed that the skeleton might be that of a mixed blood (Indian-white), or even of a white man, but a detailed study of the bones has definitely removed this impression." But later (1918:59), "there remains some persistent doubt whether it is not the skeleton of a white-Indian individual. However, all the features in which the various parts of the skeleton differ from those of an ordinary Florida Indian are features pointing toward higher or more modern development. There is no feature that would suggest even remotely an individual more ancient or anthropologically more primitive than the Indian." Hrdlička described the individual bones and illustrated some of them, including his reconstructions of "Vero Man's" skull (1918: 55–59).

All of the human and animal bones from stratum 2 and the 2/3 contact were completely and similarly fossilized. Hrdlička argued that fossilization can occur very rapidly and should not be used as a criterion for antiquity or contemporaneity. He was certain that the human remains were fairly recent burials intruded from above into the formation containing the Pleistocene animals.

The importance of the artifacts—pottery sherds, bone points and ornaments, stone points and flakes, and an "incised" proboscidian tusk—and their locations within strata 2 and 3 at Vero cannot be overstated.

At least 100 pottery sherds are reported from stratum 3 but, with one possible exception, *no* pottery came from stratum 2. A few flint spalls and bone implements, however, although scarce in stratum 3 compared to pottery, were recovered in stratum 2. In fact, Sellards mentioned that the flint spalls in stratum 2 were in excess of those from stratum 3 even though more material from stratum 3 had been handled. Nevertheless, the scientists who evaluated the evidence in 1916 concluded that the flint and bone artifacts were carried into stratum 2 via roots or burrowing animals. It seems strange that only a single piece of the more plentiful pottery worked its way downward by similar mechanisms. There is no clear description or illustration of the exact location within stratum 3 at which the sherds were found in relationship to human and animal remains or flint and bone artifacts, but Sellards (1916a: 142) may have realized that there was a significant time lapse between the base of stratum 3 (Melbourne/Van Valkenburg) and higher up (Van Valkenburg): "The position leads to the suggestion that the bones [of extinct animals] lying at the base of stratum 3 were derived from stratum no. 2. . . . It is well to remember, however, that human [artifactual] remains characterize stratum No. 3. A fact indicated by an abundance of pottery, many bone implements, arrowheads, and other small flints."

Since no flint sources exist near Vero, no one questioned that the flint material was brought from chert outcrops 100 miles to the northwest. Sellards (1916a: 138) and MacCurdy (in Sellards et al. 1917: 58) illustrate some of the flakes from stratum 2 and the base of stratum 3. They are very small and probably not utilized, but nevertheless the striking platforms and bulbs of percussion are unmistakable characteristics of humanly struck specimens. Everyone agreed. Unfortunately, these flakes are not diagnostic time markers.

A photograph of a stone point is shown in Sellards (1916a: Plate 21, Fig. 1) with the following description: "Arrowhead found in stratum No. 3, south bank 470 feet west of the bridge. Actual length of specimen 64 mm [about 2.5 inches] Florida Survey Collection No. 6927." I have been unable to locate this point, but the photograph is reproduced in Figure 1.8. It looks like a Paleoindian style. Jeffrey Mitchem and James Dunbar (personal communication, 2006) disagree that the Vero stone point is Paleoindian. Without the point, we really do not know. However, the conchoidal fracture that extends from the base toward the distal end looks very much like a flake was removed to produce a fluted object. Both Mitchem and Dunbar conclude that the "projection" in the middle of the base is a segment of a broken stem, but it may also be the remnant of a striking platform that was created to furnish purchase for the removal of the flute. The point was actually found between strata 3 and 2 "in exactly the same place as the bones of Skeleton II and in close proximity to them, if not in actual association" (Hrdlička 1918: 45). This projectile point, if relocated, is the only diagnostic artifact that could furnish indisputable evidence of the contemporaneity of humans with extinct animals at Vero.

An exception to the above statement is the "engraved" tip of a proboscidian tusk illustrated in Sellards (1916a: Plate 22, Figs. 1 and 2; Fig. 1.9). This specimen and a fragmentary bird bone, also "incised," were recovered at the base of stratum 2. The tusk is 13.3 centimeters (about 5 inches) long. Unfortunately, it seems to have disappeared. MacCurdy (in Sellards et al. 1917: 57), who studied the artifacts, did not consider the markings

Fig. 1.8. Stone point found at Vero (Sellards 1916a: Plate 21, Fig. 1). Courtesy of G. Harley Means, Florida Geological Survey.

on the tusk and on the fragment of bird bone to be the work of humans. The other bone objects from stratum 2 and the 3/2 contact were unexceptional.

The fauna in stratum 2 and probably the extinct forms at the base of stratum 3 at Vero were in primary position. And there was no possibility that there was mixing of terrestrial species from older deposits because stratum 1 (Anastasia) was laid down in a marine environment. Oliver P. Hay (in Sellards et al. 1917: 55) erroneously assigned the bones of stratum 2 to the Early or Middle Pleistocene and concluded, "The human bones appear to be of Pleistocene age. At present I perceive no other reason for doubting this than that their presence in No. 2 and No. 3 contravenes our present ideas regarding the history of the human race."

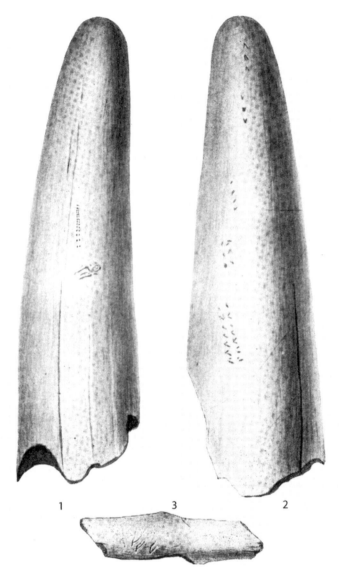

1   3   2

Fig. 1.9. Tip of proboscidian tusk found at Vero (Sellards 1916a: Plate 22).

The following comments by Sellards are interesting and years ahead of future established facts: "Man lived with and hunted *Elephas primigenius* in Europe, and it is not improbable that he may have followed the spread of that species to America" (Sellards et al. 1917: 24); "If it is true that the Cro-Magnon race of Europe of some 25,000 years ago present but few structural differences from modern Europeans, why should we doubt that the more isolated American race may have persisted through a longer period without sensible change in structure?" (Sellards 1917: 25). He concludes his study of Vero, "By these discoveries in Florida the contemporaneity of man with a Pleistocene fauna is definitely established for the first time in America" (Sellards 1916a: 160).

I will have more to say about Vero following a discussion of the Melbourne and Helen Blazes sites. Still later, I will reevaluate Vero in light of subsequent findings in the Americas.

Melbourne (8BR44 and 8BR47)

Interest in Vero lagged for a time but was revived by the discovery of fossil bones and human remains under similar conditions to Vero in the vicinity of Melbourne, about 30 miles north.

In 1922, C. P. Singleton, a Harvard zoologist, discovered an *Elephas columbi* skeleton while clearing land to plant an orange grove. The bones were exposed in the banks of a small stream (Crane Creek) winding through a palmetto hammock about a mile and a half southwest of Melbourne, Florida. The stream had been drained by the construction of a canal in the area. Frederic B. Loomis, professor of paleontology at Amherst College, Massachusetts, was employed to remove the skeleton. In December 1923, "While this skeleton was being excavated, bones and teeth of other extinct animals came to light, until an assemblage had been found which suggested that found at Vero" (Loomis 1924: 503).

A second elephant was discovered about 40 feet north, also in the banks of the stream. "In starting to take out the second individual, a pit was dug, and a large rough flint implement was found among fragments of ribs. It lay in the lower part of a bed of undisturbed sand, 36 inches below the surface" (Loomis 1924: 503; Figs. 1.10 and 1.11). In the same deposit as the flint implement, Loomis identified mammoth, mastodon, horse, sloth, tapir, peccary, camel, deer, fox, sabre-toothed cat, rabbit, alligator, turtles, birds, and fish. Three bone artifacts were recovered from the nearby canal bank in a stratum similar to that containing the stone point. In 1925, approximately 100 feet west of this location, a finely worked spearhead (Fig. 1.12, USNM 363175), a human rib, and several pieces of charcoal were found associated with teeth of Mylodon, Megalonyx, and Chlamytherium in a "fairly thin layer at the top of bed No. 2 [Melbourne Formation]. A tooth of the Mylodon lay almost in contact with the stone point" (Gidley and Loomis 1926: 260). The greater part of bed No. 3 (Melbourne–Van Valkenburg) had been removed earlier by workmen for agricultural purposes. The style of the spearhead suggests that the deposit was disturbed, mixing artifacts and bones of more recent time periods with bones of extinct animals (see Summary for another possibility concerning the origin

Fig. 1.10. Stone point found among elephant ribs at the Singleton site (BR47), near Melbourne (Loomis 1924: 505; courtesy of Laura Tayler and Amherst College, Amherst, Massachusetts).

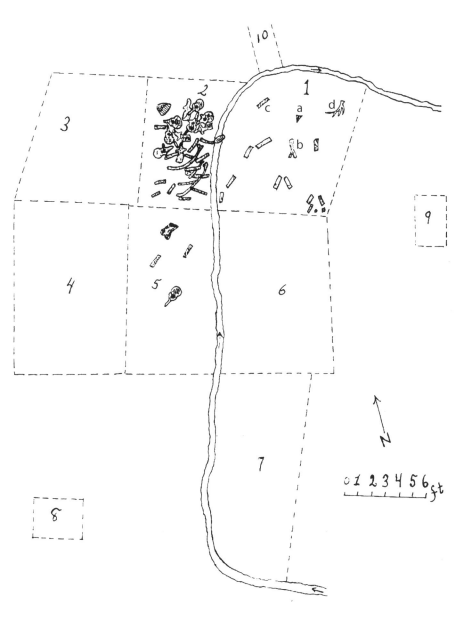

Fig. 1.11. Sketch map of excavations at the Singleton site (BR47): "Pits 1, 2, and 5 yielded bones of *Elephas columbi*, the others being barren; *a* is the arrowhead" (from Loomis 1924: 504).

1   0   5
centimeters

Fig. 1.12. Stone point found at the Singleton site (BR47), near Melbourne, in 1925 by Gidley and Loomis (1926: 260), either "planted" or displaced from more recent strata (see text). Courtesy of James Krakker, U.S. National Museum (USNM 363175).

of this artifact). The location where all these materials were recovered is called the Singleton site (BR47).

In January 1925, Dr. J. W. Gidley of the United States National Museum and Professor Loomis met at Melbourne. They examined the area together and planned a six-week Amherst-Smithsonian expedition to explore systematically the area of Crane Creek and the newly dug drainage ditch. During the expedition, which began in late June 1925, they observed fossil bones in the canal bank about 200 feet southwest of the clubhouse on the Melbourne golf course and chose that location to excavate (Golf Course site, BR 44). Stratum 3 was 18–24 inches thick and contained vegetation typical of Vero. Stratum 2, the bone bed, was 5 feet thick and rested on stratum 1, the Anastasia Formation. Within a few inches of the top of stratum 2, a crushed human skull was encountered along with pieces of finger, arm, and leg bones. A horse tooth was found near the human bones; the jaw of a tapir and bones of an extinct species of box turtle were recovered nearby.

Gidley and Loomis attempted to explain the presence of the crushed human skull in stratum 2 as an intrusion from stratum 3, "but over it lay, undisturbed, stratified material of the No. 3 bed. Thus it is evident that the skull must have come to place in No. 2 bed before No. 3 bed was laid down; . . . it is quite conceivable that it may have lain on the erosional surface between No. 2 and No. 3 beds, and have been pushed down into No. 2 bed by trampling. Therefore, the skull may be later in age than the deposition of most of No. 2 bed, and may represent the interval of time when erosion was going on. However, there are the other bones found in this same upper 6 inches that seem to belong to the fauna of No. 2 bed" (Gidley and Loomis 1926: 259).

In February 1926, Gidley returned to the Golf Course site, enlarged the pit made the previous year, and satisfied himself that the human bones actually came from the fossil stratum (Gidley 1927: 169–170). Dr. Wythe Cooke, a geologist, was sent by the U.S. Geological Survey to examine the deposits. Just prior to his arrival, a piece of ivory was discovered and replaced where found, at the base of the bone bed. The specimen was observed in its original position by Cooke, Mr. C. P. Singleton, and Dr. H. M. Ami, a geologist from Canada. None of them thought it possible that it had been intruded into the bone bed. Cooke remarked, "This fragment of ivory, possibly an artifact, had flat faces not corresponding to the natural surfaces of the tusk and marked by a more or less regular pattern of scratches. If the flat faces and scratches on this ivory are the work of human hands, man must have been in Florida from the early part of the deposition of the bone bed" (Cooke 1926: 442, 447). The whereabouts of this important object is not known.

In 1928, Gidley excavated stratum by stratum an area of the Golf Course site 100 by 30 feet. When he removed the uppermost Van Valkenburg deposit (stratum 3), he discovered basin-like depressions in the surface of the Melbourne Bone Bed (stratum 2). Gidley attributed the depressions to trampling and wallowing by animals during dry seasons when wet weather ponds dried up: "Some of the largest depressions had a depth of 2 feet or more and a width of 1–6 feet. Their structure and character show that they had been worked into the surface of bed number 2 when it was more nearly level" (Gidley 1929: 492–493).

Gidley confirmed, as observed also at Vero, that the contact zone between strata 3 and 2 represented an erosional zone with drier conditions of unknown but probably long duration:

The top of strata 2 is underlain by 12–18 inches of a dense semi-consolidated fine sand which gradually merges into the coarser, looser sand of the lower part of the bed. This upper part of the bed is so firm that lumps of it will withstand considerable handling. It is marked everywhere by numerous vertical dark streaks, evidently the remains of old roots of scrub palmetto, which seem to have covered the surface of the completed bed before the swamp was formed in which the deposits of bed number 3 were laid down. Roots of grass were also seen, particularly around the borders of some of the basin-like depressions. (Gidley 1929:492–493; see also Cooke and Mossom 1929: 220)

During the 1928 field season, Dr. Frank H. H. Roberts Jr. was sent by the Bureau of American Ethnology to view the work being done at Melbourne. He observed in situ a flint projectile point 20 inches beneath the contact plane in the bone bed near and on the same level as a mastodon bone (Fig. 1.13, USNM 342219). It is perhaps noteworthy that he had also observed in situ the skeletons of 23 bison of an extinct species with associated Folsom points at the recently discovered site (1926) near Folsom, New Mexico (Roberts 1937: 153–162).

Everyone seemed to be on the lookout for early humans. Interest in the Melbourne Bone Bed may have intensified because in 1928 remains of Peking Man, an undeniably primitive type of human called *Homo erectus*, were found in Zhoukoudien Cave near Beijing, China. Earlier finds of *Homo erectus* in the gravels of the Solo River by Dr. Eugene Dubois in 1891 were met with a vicious outcry and accusations of heresy. Dubois' *Pithecanthropus erectus* or Java Man was dismissed with contempt.

1   0   5
centimeters

Fig. 1.13. Stone point
from the Golf Course
site (BR44), near
Melbourne, in 1928
(Gidley 1929). Courtesy
of James Krakker, U.S.
National Museum
(USNM 342219).

Gidley returned in 1929 and 1930 for two months each season. In 1929, he recovered a turtle-back scraper (Fig. 1.14, USNM 342217) and a "blade" (USNM 342218), which cannot be found, in association with bear, camel, mastodon, horse, and tapir (Gidley 1930).

Helen Blazes (8BR27)

The Helen Blazes site is located in Brevard County near the headwaters of the St. Johns River, 10 miles southwest of Melbourne. The site was the topic of a doctoral dissertation at Columbia University in 1954 by William Ellis Edwards. He states, "At the Helen Blazes site (BR27), for the first time in modern archeological research east of the Great Plains, there became available potentialities of demonstrating the contemporaneity of man with fauna typical of the Pleistocene, of accurately dating 'Early Hunters'

1 0   5
|ⁱⁱⁱⁱᴵⁱⁱⁱⁱᴵ ▬▬▬ ▬▬▬
       centimeters

Fig. 1.14a, b. Turtle-back scraper from the
Golf Course site (BR44), near Melbourne, in
1929 (Gidley 1930). Courtesy of James Krakker, U.S. National Museum (USNM 342217).

1   0   5
|ⁱⁱⁱⁱᴵⁱⁱⁱⁱ ▬▬▬ ▬▬▬
        centimeters

geologically, and of demonstrating by stratigraphic evidence the priority of Paleo-Indian to Archaic cultures" (Edwards 1954: 8). Because of these claims, and because of the proximity and similarity of Helen Blazes to Vero and Melbourne, it is important to examine the unpublished data from this location.

Until the construction of the Melbourne-Tillman drainage system in 1923, all of the land surrounding the site was a marsh, submerged for a major part of each year; it is now a flat prairie. Edwards first surveyed the area in 1941 but found no evidence of "Early Man." He was more for-tunate, beginning in 1949, when the Helen Blazes site was discovered by an exploratory and drainage trench. Edwards saw in situ and recorded the exact provenience in the trench of two points and several retouched flakes. During the summers of 1950 and 1951, he excavated the equivalent of 60 five-foot squares. All of the units were dug to the sterile, jointed, sandy blue-gray clay (his stratum III). The site measured 800 feet N-S and 400 feet E-W, but the area in which artifacts and flakes were concentrated is much smaller.

Edwards identified eight strata at Helen Blazes with stratum I at the base (Fig. 1.15), although he describes an even lower deposit. Several of the strata were divided into substrata interpreted as cycles of deposition followed by weathering and erosion: "This area of Florida, with its flat to-pography and low elevation, is remarkably sensitive to fluctuations in sea level. Thus, if other factors remain fairly constant, deposition can be an-ticipated when the water table and associated sea level are approximately as high as or higher than at present. Conversely, a water table and a sea level decidedly lower than at present will result in erosion" (Edwards 1954: 55).

Strata I and II (Anastasia) are marine, stratum III is blue-gray clay, and stratum IV (white sand) was sparse or missing over most of the site. After discussing climatic and depositional conditions prevailing when strata I–IV developed, Edwards concludes that the light to dark brown sand deposits of strata V and VI were deposited along the shore of a freshwa-ter lake and are coeval with the Melbourne Bone Bed at Melbourne and Vero when the area was inhabited by a varied assemblage of extinct mam-mals. The lower part of stratum VII is equated with the Melbourne–Van

			1/2 Inch		
PARTIALLY DECOMPOSED ORGANIC MATTER				VIII C	A₀
GRAY BLACK (WHITE SAND AND HUMUS)			3	VIII B	A₁
LIGHT GRAY SAND (LESS HUMUS)			6	VIII A	A₂
MOTTLED GRAY-BROWN SAND			12	VII	G
VERY LIGHT BROWN SAND				VI B	A₂
LIGHT BROWN SAND			23 / 28	VI A	A₂₁
DARK BROWN SAND			30½ / 31	V / IV	B₁ / A₂
COLUMNAR DARK BLUE-GRAY SANDY CLAY	WHITE-CREAM SAND			III C	B₁
IRREGULARLY PRISMATIC BLUE-GRAY SANDY CLAY			39 / 43	III B	B₂
LIGHT BLUE-GREEN SANDY CLAY WITH ORANGE-YELLOW INCLUSIONS			53	III A	B₃
MARINE SHELLS, CLAY, AND SAND				II	C
COMPACT BLUE CLAY WITH SOME MARINE SHELLS			102	I	D

Fig. 1.15. Stratigraphy at the Helen Blazes site (BR27) (Edwards 1954: 25, Figure 4).

Fig. 1.16. Examples of stone points from the Helen Blazes site (BR27) (Edwards 1954: 63b, Figure 17).

Valkenburg disconformity. Upper stratum VII and stratum VIII are inter-preted as Van Valkenburg.

Strata V–VIII all contained artifacts. From strata V and VI, Edwards re-covered seven lanceolate points (Paleoindian styles; Fig. 1.16) plus several types of unifacial scrapers, gravers, and utilized flakes (Fig. 1.17). Strata V and VI contained no pottery. Upper stratum VII and stratum VIII yielded artifacts of the Archaic and Ceramic periods, but Edwards's dissertation was concerned primarily with the earlier time period.

Fig. 1.17. Examples of unifacial tools from the Helen Blazes site (BR27) (Edwards 1954: 66b, Figure 18).

Nearly all of the points illustrated in Edwards's dissertation came from stratum VI between 14 and 27 inches below surface, i.e., toward the top of the Melbourne formation but below the Melbourne–Van Valkenburg disconformity. The styles of two points are clearly Middle Archaic. One of these is listed as coming from stratum VII; the other is listed as coming from 14 inches below surface, so possibly it should also belong to VII. The other points range in appearance from Clovis to Bolen. Interestingly, while none of the spearheads came from stratum V, at least 16 of the unifacial tools came from stratum V. In all, 9 stone points, 35 tools, and 400 flakes were recovered in strata V and VI and lower VII, but no bones, shell, or charcoal survived. Therefore, Edwards's conclusion that his strata V and VI at the Helen Blazes site represent the same time period as the Melbourne Bone Bed at Vero and Melbourne is based strictly on artifact styles known to be Paleoindian.

Edwards added an important anthropological perspective to his analysis of the Helen Blazes site: "The Helen Blazes people did not represent a shellfish culture. Although some of the chert artifacts were undoubtedly utilized for work in bone or wood, most can be attributed to but one main economic activity—the utilization of game animals" (1954: 82). Further, "The undomesticated nature of the food supply limited the size of the population. Helen Blazes was a camp site occupied repeatedly but not constantly by a migratory hunting and gathering band over a long period of time. They were typical Paleoindians but they were not the only inhabitants of the Florida peninsula" (p. 83). Edwards supports this last statement by suggesting that the imported chert from 100 miles to the northwest might have been obtained during seasonal migrations, but it might also represent trade with other Paleoindian groups. He favors the second explanation and also hypothesizes that the Helen Blazes people were patrilineal and patrilocal because of the need for the male hunters to possess an intimate knowledge of the territory in which they lived. The nature of the stone remains definitely suggests a portable tool kit. No large chert nodules were recovered. It is important to note that after the inhabitants of Florida became more sedentary around 6,000 to 8,000 years ago, tools manufactured of chert are rare or absent outside of the source areas (Purdy 1981a).

Because of the small amount of surviving information, it would be easy to conclude that early Paleoindians were culturally naive. But following megafauna was not a single resource destination. We know that chert and water were also important. We do not know how extensively people were seeking other products such as wood for tools and plants for food, clothing, and containers.

I have not been able to locate the artifacts from the Helen Blazes site.

Summary, Discussion, and Update

More than 90 years ago, human skeletal remains were found in apparent association with several species of Late Ice Age animals during the construction of a drainage canal near Vero Beach. After careful examination of the evidence, E. H. Sellards, the state geologist, announced the discovery in a publication dated 1916. These and similar finds near Melbourne in the 1920s met with overenthusiastic acceptance by some investigators and outright rejection by others.

By 1916, it was a well-known fact that Florida has some of the richest fossil vertebrate deposits in the world. It was also known that humans had inhabited the state long before Europeans arrived in the sixteenth century. But, until the finds at Vero and Melbourne, no one thought that extinct animals and people coexisted. Experts from the fields of geology, paleontology, archaeology, and physical anthropology visited the sites to inspect the deposits from which the animals and humans were recovered. Each of these prominent scholars offered an objective evaluation of the situation. One-half of them concluded that humans lived in Florida at the same time as Ice Age animals, and the other half determined that the human skeletal remains were aboriginal graves dug into the ancient strata, or were deposited there by various other means. These were scientists. Why couldn't they deliver an unbiased, collaborated consensus? Because, in the early twentieth century, important supportive studies were in their infancy or lacking. For example:

- A classification system was not yet completed that clearly distinguished animals of one time period from another.

- No dating technique existed to prove that many Ice Age (Pleistocene) animals did not become extinct until approximately 12,000 years ago.
- No thorough studies had been conducted of variations in physical attributes of Native Americans through time and space.
- The various cultural periods and associated artifacts dating from Paleoindian to Historic Contact had not been identified yet.

Because of these factors, the half who dismissed the Vero finds as unfounded won out, and now, 90 years later, the issue has not been resolved. The human and animal bones from the Vero and Melbourne sites, after an initial flurry over their discovery, remain in storage in various institutions throughout the eastern United States or have been lost and forgotten.

But topics and events of great significance never become the past. The tide began to turn in 1926 after a distinctive type of spearhead was found at Folsom, New Mexico, in association with an extinct form of bison, and in 1932 at Clovis, New Mexico, when a similar type of spearhead was found with proboscidians. The significance of the differences between these two spearheads was not recognized for many years. In 1935, John C. Merriam, president of Carnegie Institution in Washington, D.C., said of his visit to Vero and Melbourne, "On the visit in 1932 and again in 1935, the impression obtained was that, at the localities visited, the occurrence of remains of certain extinct animals considered to represent a Pleistocene fauna suggests the type of association known in the Southwest, where human relics appear with a fauna now, at least in large part, extinct" (Merriam 1935). This is the same Professor Merriam who evaluated the La Brea skeleton two decades earlier (Merriam 1914).

In 1936 and 1937, "worked" bones were recovered from the Melbourne Bone Bed at the Gifford site (IR7), located about 3 miles north of Vero. Drs. A. E. Jenks and E. H. Sellards examined the bones and concluded that the markings on proboscidean and other bones appeared to have been made by flint knives in cutting slices of meat (Sellards 1940: 385). The specimens were at the University of Minnesota and in a museum at the courthouse in Jackson, Minnesota. They were transferred to the Minnesota Historical Society in 1999 (John Soderberg, personal communication, 2006).

In 1937, an international conference was convened in Philadelphia to discuss human origins (MacCurdy 1937). Two of the major actors from twenty years earlier summarized their conclusions about the antiquity of humans on the Atlantic Coast of Florida. Sellards (in MacCurdy 1937: 193–210) did not waver in his original analysis: "man reached this continent before the close of the Pleistocene and participated in the great drama of the extinction of the magnificent mammalian fauna of that period" (210).

Hrdlička (in MacCurdy 1937: 93–104) discussed his conclusions about the human remains at the Vero site and his reconstruction of the crushed skull found at Melbourne: "The Melbourne skull finally, now reconstructed, though defective, . . . is the skull of an Indian male, of advanced adult age, undeformed, brachycranic, high, and in general presenting the ordinary Florida mound Indian type and characters" (98). He still insisted that the skeletons were intentional burials intruded into the lower stratum from a more recent time period.

T. Dale Stewart, who succeeded Hrdlička at the Smithsonian, made new reconstructions of the Melbourne and Vero skulls. Whereas Hrdlička had concluded that Vero "man" was a male about 5 feet, 10 inches tall, somewhat advanced in life, robust, and similar to Algonquin or Sioux, Stewart concluded that it probably was a female and Paleoindian. He determined that the Melbourne skull was also a Paleoindian type and probably female. The crania from Vero and Melbourne are dolichocranic (long, narrow-headed) and medium vaulted compared to increased temporal fullness, broader heads, and higher cranial vaulting of Archaic and more recent periods. Stewart noted that it is rare for modern or prehistoric Florida Indians to have a cranial index below 75. Vero is 72.4 and Melbourne is 73.1. He concluded, "The similarity of form between the Vero skull and the new version of the Melbourne skull means that the latter, too, is a stranger in Florida. And both of these strangers were found 40 miles apart and in a geological stratum containing mastodon and mammoth remains. This can hardly be a coincidence" (Stewart 1946: 20).

In the early 1950s, William Ellis Edwards had the advantage of evaluating and comparing the results of his investigations at Helen Blazes to numerous recently disovered sites in Florida (e.g., Jenks and Simpson 1941; Simpson 1948) and throughout the country that contained butchered bones of extinct animals, tools and weapons manufactured from the bones of those animals, and diagnostic stone spearheads found with their skeletons. The newly introduced radiocarbon dating technique proved that these associations were ancient. By 1950, archaeologists, paleontologists, and geologists accepted that the contemporaneity of humans with extinct megafauna was indisputable. More important, this acceptance represented the liberation of a confined mental attitude and gave birth to a new paradigm. Edwards also had the advantage of utilizing the information contained in Rouse's outstanding publication (1951) about the Indian River area of Florida.

Irving Rouse, in addition to recording all sites and time periods in the vicinity of the central Atlantic Coast of Florida (Volusia, Seminole, Orange, Brevard, Osceola, Indian River, St. Lucie, and Martin counties), furnishes the most complete and objective evaluation of the controversial discoveries at Vero and Melbourne, including their relationship to climatic changes and cultural episodes (Figs. 1.18 and 1.19). He attributes the presence of human remains and artifacts in the bone bed to wells that were dug into that stratum by aboriginal peoples in search of water. Previous theories had postulated that the materials were incorporated there as a result of intentional burial, or by wallowing, trampling, burrowing by animals, or various other mechanisms. Rouse wrote:

Our study fails to support the theory that man was contemporaneous in the Indian River area with the extinct Melbourne fauna . . . [but] we would not be surprised if it were eventually proven (1951: 259–260). What is needed is the discovery of a primary site, in which the bones of extinct animals have been deposited *by the Indians* as an integral part of their refuse and show traces of the burning and cutting which are a concomitant of practically all primarily deposited refuse observed by us.

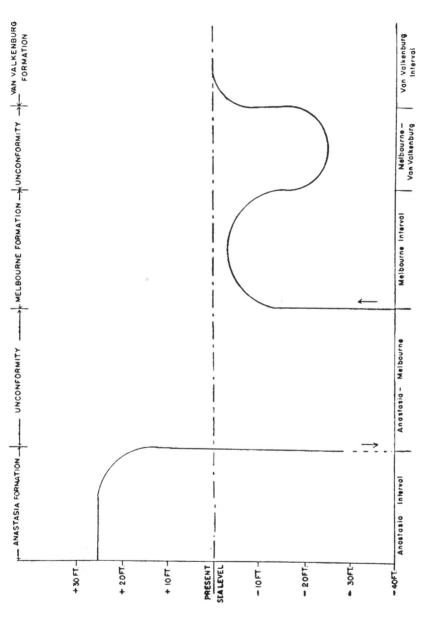

Fig. 1.18. Changes in sea level in the Indian River area as indicated by the geological formations (from Rouse 1951: 23).

Geologic Intervals	Cultural Periods[b]		Historic Periods
	Seminole		American Ascendency
			Seminole Ascendency
Van Valkenburg	?	St. Augustine	Ais Decline
			Friendship
	Malabar II		Hostility
			Exploration
	Malabar I'		
Melbourne-Van Valkenburg	Malabar I		
	Orange		
	Preceramic		
Melbourne			
Anastasia-Melbourne	—		
Anastasia			

[a] The vertical dimensions should not be taken to indicate duration, since they are not to scale.
[b] Only aboriginal culture is shown.

Fig. 1.19. Correlation of geological intervals and cultural periods (from Rouse 1951: 235).

In this respect, we disagree [with those] who state that the final decision as to the antiquity of Vero and Melbourne man must depend on geologic evidence. In our opinion, if antiquity is ever demonstrated, it will more probably be through the discovery of an *archeological* site in which the bones of extinct animals occur as a normal component of the refuse. (Rouse 1951:260)

In a perfect situation, Dr. Rouse is correct, but his view stems from his experiences at archaeological sites of more recent time periods where sealed deposits contain a large and varied inventory of durable objects that can be identified stylistically and dated by relative or absolute methods. While no aboriginal Florida culture had access to the hundreds of thousands of material items available to the average person of the twenty-first century, the sedentary populations of the Archaic and Ceramic Periods (ca. 8,000 years ago to Historic Contact in the sixteenth century) had vastly more abundance than their Late Ice Age predecessors more than 100 centuries ago. The result of sedentism alone leads to the accumulated refuse described by Rouse, although more than 90 percent of it will not survive except under very favorable conditions. Nomadic Ice Age people left little garbage, and almost none of it survived. In cases where extinct animal bones and human skeletal material are commingled, the bones are fossilized and thus undatable by the radiocarbon technique.

Rouse knew of the initial work being conducted at the Helen Blazes site by William Edwards; he mentions in a footnote that Edwards had "found several Suwannee points (shaped like Folsom) . . . which, if substantiated, may well be associated with the Melbourne interval" (Rouse 1951: 260). Unfortunately, Edwards's dissertation was never published, and its contents have been buried in the archives for 50 years.

In 1956 and 1957, Weigel (1963) returned to the Vero site to study the smaller vertebrates, which were little known, and to review a number of other species whose taxonomic status was uncertain. He verified the stratigraphy as previously established. He mentioned that the contact between Bed 2 (Melbourne bone bed) and Bed 3 (Van Valkenburg) represented an interval of erosion and is sharply demarcated. He found flint flakes, but no human bones, toward the top of Bed 2. Mammoth, mastodon, sloth, horse, and tapir occurred in the same level where a radiocarbon sample of charcoal dated 30,000 was taken near the base of Bed 2 overlying the shell marl (Anastasia). As far as I am aware, this is the only radiocarbon date that exists from deep within the Melbourne Formation.* More recent dates were received for samples higher in the deposits. Weigel makes the interesting observation that the percentage of now-extinct mammals decreased from 50 percent at the bottom of Bed 2 to only 5 percent at the top of Bed 2. Further research might determine if this situation is more than an isolated incidence.

The drainage canals of Florida can be equated to arroyo cutting in the western United States where a deeply buried extinct fauna have been found unquestionably in association with artifacts. People are still collecting bones in the vicinity of Vero and Melbourne, but nothing professional is going on. A well-designed project incorporating the expertise of individuals from various disciplines using twenty-first-century techniques might resolve this long-debated issue. Gidley (1929: 498) said that the burden of proof rests on the dissenters, but I believe it is the responsibility of the *pros* to prove to the *cons* that Florida was not devoid of the species *Homo sapiens* when elephants still roamed here. After all, the truth is in the proof.

*Converse (1973: 3) reported a radiocarbon date of 21,150±400 years for a section of mastodon rib from the center of a site in Palm Beach County a short distance south of Vero.

2

Early Paleoindian Period in Florida, ca. 14,000 Years Ago

I am going to restrict my discussion of Paleoindian in Florida to

- The Late Glacial period.
- A specific stone weapon type called Clovis and its possible contemporaries Suwannee and Simpson (Fig. 2.1a, b, c).
- A big game hunting way of life.
- The presence of now-extinct Ice Age animals, a few of which were butchered or their bones or tusks made into artifacts.

These criteria differ from typical models of Paleoindian in Florida, which include divisions of Early, Middle, and Late. The Middle and Late Paleoindians were probably still primarily hunters, but vast climatic changes had occurred with the retreat of the last glacier. These people were manufacturing slightly different types of stone weapons, were hunting all modern fauna, becoming generalized, and spreading into previously uninhabited niches following the emergence of a more amenable environment that did not confine them to river and spring resources as seems to be true for the Early Paleoindians.

Clovis belongs to a continent-wide manifestation of the elements listed above for the Early Paleoindians of Florida. The Clovis point was first discovered in the early 1930s but was not named or distinguished from other early types until many years later. For a recent summary of the sequence of events, see Dixon (1999: 1–17). As has been said by many authors, the unmistakable attributes of the Clovis point and its association with extinct fauna (especially mammoth and mastodon), mostly located at ancient water sources, indicate that it dispersed rapidly across North America and became incorporated into already existing cultures, much as the com-

(a)

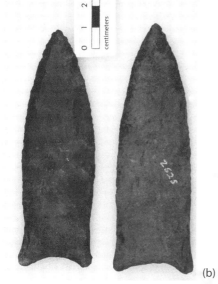

Fig. 2.1. (a) Clovis, (b) Suwannee,
(c) Simpson points (courtesy of
Alvin Hendrix).

(b)

(c)

puter has done today. This rapid spread is supported by radiocarbon dates that place Clovis between 12,300 and 11,600 RCYBP (radiocarbon years before present), or about 14,000 years ago (see Dating below). Another argument, with equal support, is that there were no humans in the Western Hemisphere until the Clovis people burst downward and outward from locations east of the Bering Strait as soon as climatic conditions permitted.

Dating

Until 1949, no method existed whereby archaeological materials could be dated, except relatively: that is, by assuming that deeper deposits were older than those above them, or that certain artifacts styles were older or younger than others based on a technique called seriation. Radiocarbon analysis made it possible for the first time to date organic remains as old as 50,000 years (Arnold and Libby 1949). The archaeological profession benefited most from this discovery. The principle upon which radiocarbon dating is based has been described in numerous publications (e.g., Purdy 1996: 138–140). All living organisms (plants and animals) maintain a constant amount of radioactive carbon (carbon 14) that disintegrates at a known rate after an organism dies. The rate of decay is determined by the half-life of carbon 14, which Libby estimated to be 5,568 years. This figure is still used even though 5,730 years is more accurate. This simply means that one-half of the radioactive carbon decays every 5,730 years after the death of a plant or animal. The sample size needed for analysis was often prohibitive until another technique was developed called accelerator mass spectrometer (AMS) that requires only a few milligrams in order to obtain a radiocarbon age.

Radiocarbon analysis assumes that the proportion of radioactive unstable carbon 14 to stable carbon 12 has remained virtually constant in the earth's atmosphere throughout a 50,000- year period. But all is not perfect. Proxy data furnish conflicting conclusions about the accuracy of radiocarbon results and thus about the time that certain events occurred in the past. Proxies denote pieces of evidence derived through indirect means. Fluctuations in the proportion of C-14 to C-12 result from variation in cosmic radiation reaching the upper atmosphere. For example, during the cool phase of the last glacial recession, the atmosphere became supercharged with C-14, which yielded radiocarbon dates that were too young. (See Dunbar 2002 and his references for a clear discussion of the significance of proxy evidence when applied to paleoclimate.)

The first hint of a discrepancy came from dendrochronology. Dendrochronology, or tree ring dating, furnishes a year-by-year record almost as accurate as a calendar. When tree ring counts were calibrated to radiocarbon results, it was determined that cosmic radiation and the geomagnetic field had fluctuated through time. Sometimes radiocarbon dates are nearly synchronous with dendrochronology, but other times they may be off by many hundreds of years. Radiocarbon dating laboratories provide calibration of samples along with a graph to illustrate the relationship between radiocarbon and calendar ages. Tree rings, however, do not extend far enough into the past to date some items and events of interest. Discrepancies have been identified also in ice cores and deep-sea cores.

You may wonder why these more accurate methods are not utilized in place of radiocarbon dating. Proxy data are important, but at present there is a need for further precision, correlation, and agreement about marine, terrestrial, and ice core records. In addition, it is important to realize that there is a lag between climatic events and environmental responses to the events (Dunbar 2002: 12, 27).

Other problems and possible solutions to dating organic materials and geologic deposits containing archaeological specimens are discussed in later sections.

Climate and Geology

Until recently, the Pleistocene (Ice Ages or Quaternary) referred to four stages of glacial advance and four stages of glacial recession (interglacials). In the Western Hemisphere, the glacial stages were called Nebraskan, Kansan, Illinoian, and Wisconsinan, with the last named being the youngest. The interglacial stages were called Aftonian, Yarmouthian, Sangamonian, and Holocene or Recent (present climatic conditions). Geologists now recognize more than twenty glacial episodes during the 1.86

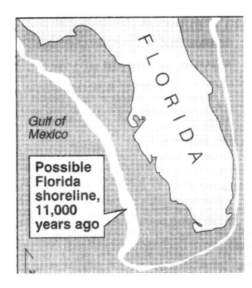

Fig. 2.2. Map of Florida showing possible location of coastline when sea level was about 100 meters lower than today.

million years of the Pleistocene (James S. Dunbar, personal communication, 2006; Martini et al. 2001; Shackleton and Opdyke 1973).

Because the Wisconsin is recognized as the fourth and final major glaciation, and is known to have lasted from approximately 50,000 to 12,000 years ago, there is a tendency to ignore or downplay the significance of advances (stadials) and retreats (interstadials) that occurred within that time period. It turns out that these intervals are extremely important in discovering and clarifying the movements and activities of animals and humans.

There are dramatic, worldwide sea level (eustatic) changes when glaciers advance and retreat. Sea level, for example, was approximately 100 meters lower than present several times during the Late Wisconsin. This situation impacted Florida in major ways. The peninsula became part of a broad coastal plain with a glacial shoreline that nearly doubled the state's land area and created a savannah corridor which animals and humans could traverse (Fig. 2.2). In addition, because of Florida's intimate relationship with the sea, sea level changes affect the groundwater level for a considerable distance inland from the coast (Webb 1974). For example, 12,000 years ago, the water level in Little Salt Spring, Sarasota County, was 30 meters (90 feet) lower than present. An understanding of eustatic/hydrologic fluctuations is critical to investigations of animals and people in Late Ice Age Florida. Fortunately, compared to other regions, reconstructions of eustatic/hydrologic fluctuations in Florida during the time period of the last Ice Age are not complicated by the need to adjust for extreme vertical movements of the land surface as a result of subsidence, earthquakes, or volcanic activity.

As mentioned, Florida was underwater from about 65 million years ago until 15 to 20 million years ago, a situation which resulted in limestone deposits that are thousands of feet thick blanketing the state. Rain and groundwater dissolve limestone, and a distinct landscape called *karst* develops. Karst topography consists of sinkholes, springs, caves, underwater river channels, and caverns. It is because these solution features exist in Florida that the story of human presence and extinct Ice Age animals can be told.

Background and History of Discoveries

An ideal archaeological site consists of

- Stratigraphy with multiple undisturbed layers easily distinguished from each other by changes in color and texture.
- Preserved and datable flora and fauna.
- Diagnostic artifacts with the oldest recovered from the lowest cultural deposit.
- Written records from Historic Period sites that can be used to supplement the archaeological record.

The absence of all or most of these components at the locations to be discussed has made it necessary for investigators to resort to innovative and ingenious means to demonstrate that people and Late Pleistocene megafauna coexisted in Florida. On the positive side, Clovis points and modified bones of extinct animals have been recovered, including artifacts of elephant ivory. Also, although still controversial, human skeletal remains have been found in association with Late Ice Age fauna.

By the late nineteenth century, it was a well known fact that many of Florida's rivers abounded with the bones of ancient animals (Sellards 1916c:

77–120). George Gaylord Simpson may have been the first to publish an account of artifacts recovered from the rivers, specifically the Ichetucknee:

> The Ocala limestone is here at or near the surface, but in places there is a shallow layer of soil and in the bed of the river there is deep muck or ooze. It is said that three skeletons of mastodons were found in this river 35 or 40 years ago. . . . Recently J. Clarence Simpson of High Springs has made a considerable collection of artifacts from the Itchatucknee [sic] River. The method of collecting is to wait until the water is low, then to wade about in the ooze until the bare feet encounter some hard object which may be recovered. In addition to arrow heads, some extraordinary awls or points of bone, apparently fossilized, were found, and also various remains of extinct animals. (Simpson 1930: 1)

According to Jenks and Simpson (1941), the "extraordinary awls or points of bone" were recovered in 1927 by the H. H. Simpson family, and at least one of them was made of elephant ivory. They were found "about a mile and one-quarter below the springs in a section . . . where the water was about four feet deep. In that short section were also found several hundred chipped stone and bone artifacts . . . [and] bones of some twenty species of extinct animals" (pp. 314–315). Jenks and Simpson compare the beveled artifacts from the Ichetucknee River to the beveled artifacts from Clovis, New Mexico.

J. Clarence Simpson (1948), in the first issue of *The Florida Anthropologist*, furnishes an excellent update on the "Folsom-like" points and ivory artifacts (Fig. 2.3a) from Florida, most of which were in the Simpson family collections. (J. Clarence Simpson was the son of Mr. and Mrs. H. H. Simpson but was not related to George Gaylord Simpson.) Clarence Simpson uses the term "Folsom-like" for the Florida specimens instead of "fluted points" because they lacked the characteristic groove of Folsom. It is interesting to note that in 1948 the significance of the differences between Clovis and Folsom had not yet been recognized. The specimens illustrated on page 12 of his article closely resemble Clovis or Suwannee;

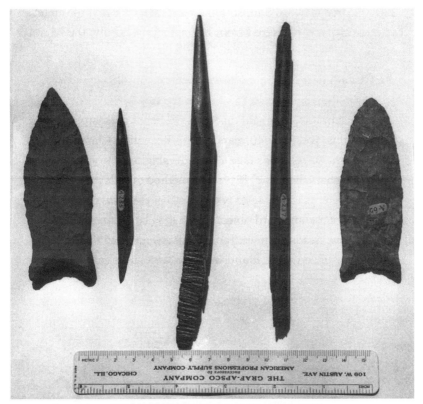

Fig. 2.3a. Stone, bone, and ivory objects recovered by Clarence Simpson around 1927 (courtesy of the Florida Geological Survey).

in fact, typical Folsom points are virtually unknown in Florida. Simpson discusses the association of the stone points, ivory tools, and extinct animals at various places in the rivers. He mentions also the presence of the clubhead (bola stone, dimple stone) at these localities and states that it is not known from more recent horizons (Fig. 2.3b).

The exact time relations of the Folsom-like points from Florida to the geologically dated Folsom sites in the west is not known. The typological relations of the artifacts, together with the association with extinct fauna would seem to indicate a rough contemporaneity. Another point of interest lies in the fact that the Folsom culture is usually looked on as oriented towards a plains type of hunting. This is not inconsistent with the Florida picture; there are a large number of plains type animals found in the Ichetucknee and Santa Fe Rivers, and Florida during this time probably resembled the game fields of Africa. (Simpson 1948: 14–15)

Simpson was hesitant to claim that the artifacts and extinct animals in Florida were contemporaneous because they were not found in geologically datable strata and because radiocarbon analysis was not yet available. The shallow limestone-paved rivers contained not only the look-alike "Folsom" points but also more recent stone points, pottery, and even beer bottles.

Surely there were other people besides the Simpsons living in Florida prior to the 1950s who collected stone points from rivers and noted their association with extinct fauna. Such finds must be buried in attics.

Simpson's 1948 article apparently stimulated some activity. John M. Goggin spent two days of a summer field school in 1949 excavating a 50-foot-long trench at the Suwannee site (8SU2) located "within the junction of the Suwannee and Santa Fe Rivers." This was a terrestrial site with

Fig. 2.3b. Examples of clubheads (aka bola, dimple, or egg stones) (courtesy of Alvin Hendrix).

limited and possibly disturbed stratigraphy; a clay hardpan was encountered at depths from 16 to 48 inches (Goggin 1950). Nevertheless, several artifacts were found that resembled Paleoindian types, and Goggin
recognized them as the Suwannee points described by Simpson in 1948.
Goggin compared 9SU2 to the Whitehurst site (8AL35) located on the
south edge of Paynes Prairie in Alachua County and named the artifacts
from both areas the Santa Fe lithic complex of the Archaic Tradition, a
designation that is no longer used. These and other terrestrial sites, e.g.,
the stratified site at Silver Springs (Neill 1958), Bolen Bluff (Bullen 1958),
the Johnson Lake stone workshop site (Bullen and Dolan 1959), and the
Darby and Hornsby Springs sites (Dolan and Allen 1961), yielded early
style projectile points and other tools but no animal bones in the upland
locations of excavations (see also Bullen 1969: 36). Suwannee and other
lanceolate-style points dredged from Tampa Bay offered further indication of Paleoindian presence in Florida (Warren 1966, 1968; see Goodyear
et al. 1983 for a summary), but again with no reported faunal remains in
direct association.

Meanwhile, paleontologists had continued to make strides collecting
and classifying the many varieties of animals. They paid little heed to the
association of the megafauna with artifacts, nor did they care about a
precisely dated time frame because the animals had already been identified as Rancholabrean, 12,000–50,000 years old. As early as 1916, E. H.
Sellards mentioned that these late Pleistocene animals had been recovered
in the Peace River, Caloosahatchee River, Sarasota Bay, Wakulla Springs,
Withlacoochee River, all along the Atlantic Coast, and near Ocala (Sellards 1916c: 100–107).

When scuba equipment became available following World War II, diving in rivers, springs, and shipwrecks to collect whatever looked interesting became a popular pastime. Everything was recovered: human skulls,
Folsom-like points, mastodon teeth, gold and silver lost by the Spanish in
the sixteenth and seventeenth centuries, and more. Some of these hobbyists became competent avocational archaeologists and paleontologists.
Ben I. Waller, Alvin Hendrix, Roger Alexon, Richard Ohmes, Don Ser-
bousek, William R. Royal, Jarl Malwin, and Guy Marwick are legendary
figures. They generously shared, or tried to share, their observations and

collections with state, museum, and university personnel. Ben Waller's contributions were among the earliest of the scuba era. He made his first regulator in 1949 out of a Maxwell House coffee can using instructions from a *Popular Science* magazine (Waller 1983).

After twenty years of diving and collecting in Florida rivers (Santa Fe, Suwannee, Oklawaha, Chipola, Withlacoochee, Wekiva, Aucilla), Waller (1970) presented a predictive model of locations where kill sites might be found—not just Paleoindian but more recent time periods as well: "The game trail crosses shallow water presenting the hunter with an opportunity to ambush his prey while its movements are restricted by the water. It also presents the Indian with the opportunity to float his victim down stream to a ledge where he can begin his butchering" (p. 131). Waller states, for example, that of 22 locations on the Santa Fe River, 18 have a set of physical conditions that fit the predictive model. (See also Waller 1969.)

Seldom did the archaeologists and paleontologists work together or respond to the amateur collectors. Waller (1983: 31–39) gives a brief history of the subject including his occasional frustration. For instance, he recovered four Suwannee points in 1963 among bones of extinct horse at the junction of the Suwannee and Santa Fe rivers; on another occasion, four inches of a Clovis point were found with elephant remains in the Waccasassa River. He tried to get a professional to come to the sites, but nobody came. Around 1970, Waller investigated the Guest Mammoth site in the Silver Springs Run, Marion County. After finding mammoth jaws and bone pins, he stopped working until an archaeologist could take over. It was almost three years before Charles A. Hoffman of Northern Arizona University arrived with field school students to begin excavations (Hoffman 1983: 83). They were not scuba divers. Most Florida archaeologists at the time were focused on other research interests. They devoted very little time to the Paleoindian period, or they included it as part of other projects. Sometimes there was disagreement between professionals and amateurs as, for example, the well-known antagonism between John M. Goggin (1962) and William R. Royal (1978) about Little Salt Spring and Warm Mineral Springs (see below).

Ripley P. Bullen worked exceptionally well with the public. He visited and excavated sites of all time periods around the state of Florida and often included landowners and collectors as coauthors of his many publications. As early as 1949, Bullen reported the recovery of a Paleoindian-style stone point from a site in Alachua County. He compiled *A Guide to the Identification of Florida Projectile Points* (1968, revised 1975), which is still used today. Illustrations on pages 50–57 accurately depict Paleoindian-style lanceolates with a brief account of their ages, measurements, and distributions as known at that time. Farr (2006) presents a reevaluation of Bullen's typology for the early periods of Florida's prehistory.

Bullen, Webb, and Waller (1970) reported the occurrence of a worked vertebral spine of a mammoth from the Santa Fe River (Fig. 2.4a, b). Waller had collected the specimen from a pothole (solution pipe) recognized in the University of Florida Fossil Vertebrate Locality Catalogue as Santa Fe IA. This publicaton appears to be the beginning of serious cooperation and respect between avocational collectors and museum, state, and university archaeologists and paleontologists.

S. David Webb's influential edited publication *Pleistocene Mammals of Florida* (1974) contains a chapter by Martin and Webb about the faunal assemblage from Devil's Den, Levy County (pp. 114–145). In a section of that chapter titled "Extinct Animals in Possible Association with Man," Martin and Webb state, "It should be noted that if the hominid remains can indeed be associated with the fossil material, the following extinct forms would be among the animal associates: mastodon, horse, extinct peccary, sabre-toothed tiger, ground sloth, dire wolf, North American spectacled bear, and bog lemming" (pp. 137–138).

In 1977, James S. Dunbar, a recent graduate from the University of Florida (1975) employed by the Division of Archives, History, and Records Management (now the Division of Historical Resources), teamed up with Ben Waller to compile a distribution map and analysis of Paleoindian sites in Florida (Dunbar 1991; Dunbar and Waller 1983; Waller and Dunbar 1977). Since 1977, Dunbar has played a major role in Paleoindian research in Florida and has been instrumental in bringing avocational collectors and professionals together.

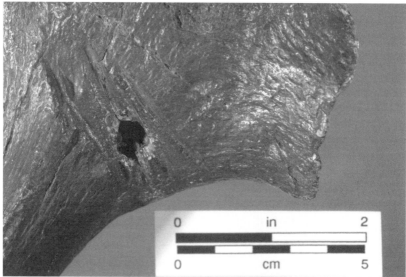

Fig. 2.4a, b. Vertebral spine of mammoth with cut marks (photo by Jeff Gage, courtesy of the Florida Museum of Natural History).

Finally, in 1981, Roger Alexson, accompanied by Bill Mathen and Bob Gingery, recovered a portion of *Bison* skull from the Wacissa River in Jefferson County with a fragment of a projectile point protruding from the frontal-parietal area (Fig. 2.5a, b). The skull was dated by radiocarbon at approximately 11,000 years B.P. (Webb et al. 1983, 1984). This discovery "galvanized both archaeologists and paleontologists to greater efforts. . . . Thus the first *Bison* kill in eastern North America stimulated a more intensive effort to investigate Florida's late Pleistocene prehistory" (Webb and Hemmings 2001: 2).

The Proof

Information relating to Late Ice Age human/megafauna interactions in Florida comes from springs, rivers, sinkholes, offshore dredged areas, and terrestrial sites. Each of these environmental settings adds important supporting evidence that, when studied collectively, leaves little doubt that these associations existed.

Springs, Spring Runs, and Adjacent Uplands

There are more than 700 recorded springs in Florida with an average flow (discharge) ranging from greater than 100 cubic feet per second (1st magnitude) to less than 1 pint per minute (8th magnitude). In addition, there are numerous undocumented and unrecorded offshore springs awaiting investigation that may have provided resources to prehistoric people and wildlife. Springs and spring runs were not as plentiful during Paleoindian times. They have increased since the end of the Pleistocene as a result of changing climatic conditions. A map showing the distribution of springs throughout the state and a glossary of terms relating to karst features (including a definition of *spring*) are given in the excellent publication *Springs of Florida* (Scott et al. 2004) (Fig. 2.6).

The underwater world of Florida's springs was virtually unknown until scuba gear became available. Even with modern technology, it is menacing to dive into what often seems like a dark bottomless pit. Descriptions in the following paragraphs are limited to a few locations where artifacts of Late

(a)

Fig. 2.5. a, *Bison antiquus* skull with lanceolate point; b, closeup (courtesy of S. David Webb and the Florida Museum of Natural History).

(b)

Fig. 2.6. Dr. Thomas M. Scott diving in Silver Springs, Marion County (courtesy of Gary Maddox, Florida Department of Environmental Protection).

Ice Age date have been recovered along with bones of extinct fauna (see Fig. 1.2).

Wakulla Springs

Wakulla Springs is a 1st magnitude spring and one of the largest and most dramatic of Florida's springs. The spring pool is roughly circular with a diameter of 315 feet (95 meters) north to south and a maximum pool depth of 185 feet (56.4 meters). Along with a few smaller springs, it gives rise to the Wakulla River (Scott et al. 2004:318; Fig. 2.7). Louis D. Tesar and B. Calvin Jones present an encyclopedic narrative of past and recent discoveries at Wakulla Springs (8WA24) and an adjacent stratified upland area

Fig. 2.7. View of Wakulla Springs and vicinity (courtesy of Tom Scott, Florida Geological Survey).

Fig. 2.8. Diver recovering a mastodon jaw from Wakulla Springs around 1930 (courtesy of the Florida Geological Survey).

(8WA329): "Wakulla Springs is famous for the crystal clear water flowing from its main spring and for the remains of Pleistocene megafauna and early Native American artifacts" (Tesar and Jones 2004:1). Their report is the primary source for this summary.

Sellards (1916c: 103) states that in the late nineteenth century, a partial skeleton of a proboscidian was removed from Wakulla Springs but was lost when the ship transporting it was destroyed off the Florida Keys. He also mentions the recovery of other mastodon or mammoth bones from the spring by a Mr. John L. Thomas. In the winter of 1930–1931, the remains of a nearly complete mastodon skeleton were recovered and reassembled (Fig. 2.8). Today, this specimen is on display at the Museum of Florida History in Tallahassee.

No formal archaeological investigations of the main spring have been undertaken although hundreds of dives into the Wakulla Springs cave system took place in the middle to late 1950s. Enormous tusks, charred wood, and over 600 completely mineralized bone projectile points were found about 300 feet back in a horizontal cavern at a depth of about 200 feet (Olsen 1958). Although these bone "pins" are not diagnostic time markers, they tinkle like glass chimes when they touch. Mammoth, mastodon, horse, tapir, camel, bison, giant armadillo, and ground sloth were identified as part of the Late Pleistocene faunal assemblage. Cultural material consisted of bone and ivory pins, bone fishhooks, Bolen points, and flint scrapers. Paleoindian artifacts have not been recovered in direct association with extinct fauna in the spring, but one Clovis point and several Suwannee points were found in or around the spring. In 1989, the Department of Anthropology, Florida State University, conducted a class on basic research diving and mapping in Wakulla Springs. Only 15 prehistoric artifacts were found; none was Paleoindian. Two other underwater field schools were conducted at 8WA24 in 1998 and 1999, but very few prehistoric artifacts were found. It was suggested that the underlying consolidated bed of calcitic mud might contain artifacts in primary or stratigraphic context.

In 1994, when construction of a 1.5-meter-deep sewer line trench began in the upland area (8WA329) near the historic Wakulla Springs lodge, B. Calvin Jones supervised archaeological investigations to determine the horizontal and vertical extent of cultural components to be affected by the construction. From previous years of testing, Jones was aware that deep stratified deposits existed at the site and that the most culturally significant material would be discovered along the north side of the lodge near its northeastern corner. At 103–105 centimeters below surface, a large Simpson preform (>10,000 years) was encountered. A Clovis-like point was found at 115 centimeters in another excavation unit (see Tesar and Jones 2000, 2004 for details). In all, 36 Paleoindian artifacts, excluding waste flakes and most expedient tools, were recovered during the project; of these, 26 came from stratigraphically undisturbed levels. The stone (chert/flint) seems to have been obtained locally, primarily from glass-like translucent St. Marks Formation chert quarries (Tesar and Jones 2004: 134).

Given the nature of the soils at terrestrial sites such as Wakulla Springs (8WA329), organic materials never survive unless calcined. The rare discovery of several pounds of burned bone at 150 centimeters below surface in 1994 originally appeared to be the remains of a food preparation pit. The oval-shaped pit, 50–60 centimeters in diameter, was capped by red ochre and extended to about 2 meters deep. In analyzing the bone, Dr. David N. Dickel (Division of Historical Resources, Tallahassee) identified the very fragmented and calcined remains of a child approximately nine years old. Deer and bird bones were also present. The red ochre, the calcined bones, and the remains of what seemed to be post molds, led Jones to the conclusion that a crematory pit had been found, but the absence of ashes indicated to him that cremation had taken place elsewhere. Since the calcined bones contained no collagen, associated materials were submitted to the Center for Applied Isotope Studies at the University of Georgia for radiocarbon analysis by AMS. The calibrated date for the cremation feature (Feature 7) is between 10,577–10,287 calendar years before present (9310±40 RCYBP to 8680±40 RCYBP). This is the oldest documented human burial in Northwest Florida (see Tesar and Jones 2004 for greater detail).

Although various archaeological projects were carried out for ten years at the Wakulla Springs Lodge site, it was only in 1994 and 1995 that excavations extended below 50–60 centimeters—deep enough to encounter Paleoindian strata. This is a good lesson to be remembered during future investigations. Another point worth considering is that excavations should be planned to answer specific questions about Paleoindian cultures in contrast to collecting data about all time periods.

Paleoindian-style stone points, ivory and bone tools, and a multitude of extinct fauna were recovered in Wakulla Springs and the spring run. It is unfortunate that the individuals who dove there did not observe artifacts in association with the animal bones or note the presence of cut marks. Nevertheless, the data from 8WA329 furnish strong supporting evidence that, during the Late Pleistocene, humans and extinct animals visited Wakulla Springs and its surrounding area at the same time.

Darby and Hornsby Springs

Darby and Hornsby Springs are both 1st magnitude springs located in northwest Alachua County near the Santa Fe River. In 1951 and 1952, excavations at the Darby and Hornsby Springs sites were funded by the Florida

Geological Survey and carried out by William Ellis Edwards, J. Clarence Simpson, and others. The work at the sites was not analyzed and reported for nearly ten years (Dolan and Allen 1961), probably because Simpson died in March 1952 and Edwards was writing his dissertation about the Helen Blazes site. Edwards had been hired by Herman Gunter (Sellards's successor as state geologist) in the 1950s to write about the excavations, but he never produced a report. It is apparent that Gunter eventually gave up and employed Dolan and Allen to do it (Jeffrey M. Mitchem, personal communication, 2006).

The Darby and Hornsby Springs sites are large lithic (chert) workshops. Bulldozing activities in the area had greatly disturbed both sites prior to excavations in 1951. There was no stratigraphy near the springs because the limestone was close to the surface. The investigators moved to higher ground and dug 5-foot test squares, 56 at Hornsby and 36 at Darby in 6-inch arbitrary levels. Most of the materials recovered were not diagnostic either temporally or spatially. Some Paleoindian-style points (Suwannee) were found in varying levels but primarily in deeper strata (>54 inches). (See, for example, Dolan and Allen 1961: 92–93, Plate VIIf, g, h.)

Hornsby Spring has a circular pool measuring 155 feet (47.2 meters) north to south, 147 feet (44.8 meters) east to west, and 34.5 feet deep (10.5 meters). The spring run is 0.9 miles (1.5 kilometers) long, 15 feet (4.6 meters) wide, and up to 5 feet (1.5 meters) deep, and it flows westward into the Santa Fe River (Scott et al. 2004: 39). Seventeen exceptionally well developed solution pipes were excavated in the Hornsby Spring run. Fifteen of them contained evidence of the association of worked lithic materials and Pleistocene animals such as horse, mastodon, and mammoth. (Scott et al. [2004: 354] define *solution sinkhole* as a "sinkhole formed by the slow subsidence of soil or sediment as the upper surface of the underlying, water-soluble sediment or rock is removed by dissolution." *Cover-collapse sinkhole* and *cover-subsidence sinkhole* are similar terms [p. 350].)

In one of the "potholes," there was a definite physical association of fossilized mastodon remains and worked lithic material. The associated materials were found in a sandy muck pocket within a solution tube of the limestone. The muck was completely enclosed within a deposit of the marl dated by radiocarbon at 9880±270. This is the latest possible date at which

Mastodon tooth with
scraper in matrix

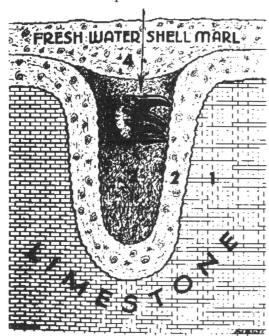

Fig. 2.9. Diagrammatic cross-section of a solution pipe filled by shell marl and noncalcareous quartz sand containing Pleistocene vertebrates and worked lithic materials (from Dolan and Allen 1961:13, Fig. 4; courtesy of the Florida Geological Survey, Tallahassee).

this lithic-skeletal physical association could have taken place (Dolan and Allen 1961: 13) (Fig. 2.9).

An underwater cave system has been mapped at Hornsby Spring. Unlike the solution pockets, no extinct megafauna or Paleoindian artifacts have been reported from either Darby or Hornsby Springs. Nevertheless, it was because of the springs and the easy procurement of stone material that people congregated there from ancient times to the present. The combination of information from the excavated upland areas and from the solution pockets leaves little doubt that these visits had already begun by the Late Pleistocene.

Devil's Den

Devil's Den (8LV84) is not a spring in true geologic terms because it does not flow onto the surface. It is a collapse feature called a *karst window* that exposes subterranean flow creating a perfect trap for the accumulation of fossils (G. Harley Means, personal communication, 2005; Scott et al. 2004: 352).

The only published report about the Devil's Den site near Williston in Levy County is by Robert A. Martin and S. David Webb (Webb 1974: 114–145). They identified 47 kinds of mammals, including *Homo sapiens*, plus a considerable diversity of fish, amphibians, reptiles, and bird fossils. Other than mention that the human bones appear to belong to the same time period as the other mammals (see Background and History of Discoveries above), Martin and Webb offer no further information about them.

Dr. John M. Goggin along with at least 14 other individuals explored Devil's Den from February 14 to November 25, 1960. Dive logs on file at the Bureau of Archaeological Research indicate there were at least 94 dives on the site (James S. Dunbar, personal communication, 2006). I have not been able to locate copies of the unpublished reports referred to by Martin and Webb. According to them, Dr. H. K. Brooks studied the geology and stratigraphy of the site. Four lateral passages lead off from the main sinkhole at depths ranging from 5 to 90 feet below the current average water level. The third passage, called chamber 3, is about 70 feet deep and produced nearly all of the fossils. Systematic collections were made from the floor of chamber 3 as well as from two crevices to the north and south of the chamber; material was also collected from the entrance to the passageway. Three stratigraphic levels were recognized in chamber 3: S is a blackened surface layer only a few centimeters deep, Y is a thicker, yellowish layer, and below Y is an unconsolidated layer of yellowish limestone debris that contained no fossils and was not given a letter designation (Martin and Webb 1974: 115).

Carl J. Clausen analyzed the archaeological remains from Devil's Den and reported his findings at the 1964 annual meeting of the Society for American Archaeology. In his master's thesis about another site, he says: "At Devil's Den, an almost perfect animal trap, several species of extinct fauna were found in association with human skeletal and cultural remains. Fluorine tests indicate the association of the extinct fauna and human skeletal material may be valid [analysis by B. J. Snell, Black Laboratories, to Dr. C. E. Ray, August 24, 1962]. The cultural material includes several varieties of bone pins and awls, a piece of ground sedimentary rock and large stemmed points" (Clausen 1964: 35). The present whereabouts of these artifacts is not known. Clausen cites a 1963 "Proposal for Continued Work at Devil's Den" and states that the manuscript is in his possession. Martin and Webb describe the fauna found in Devil's Den including the numerous skeletal elements recovered of each animal. They conclude, "Devil's Den time is the coldest time period recorded in north Florida's Pleistocene history," and "a considerable group of the most abundant species indicate open woodland of a xeric nature" (Martin and Webb 1974: 120, 134). None of the fossil bones studied showed evidence of human predation. The only animal that did not belong chronologically to the assemblage was a modern species of pig (*Sus scrofa* Linnaeus). Its poorly mineralized condition and flaky surface also suggest that it did not accumulate with the rest of the fossil material (p. 133). Romantic speculation would have this pig falling into the "cenote" while trekking across Florida with Hernando de Soto in 1539.

While the animal bones were analyzed thoroughly, the human bones were not examined at all—and still have not been analyzed (2006). Around 1970 (?), Carl Clausen gave them to Dr. Charles F. Merbs at Arizona State University. He and Dr. Donald H. Morris were involved at the time in studying the human remains from Little Salt Spring and Warm Mineral Springs. In a letter dated December 16, 2003, Merbs states:

I don't know much about the Devil's Den skeletal material. It was given to me to study by Carl Clausen, but I do not believe any studies were actually done. This was at a time when my primary interest was in Little Salt Spring and the associated burial area, and Don Morris' interest was in Warm Mineral Springs. When Little Salt didn't get funded, ASU's interest in Florida material quickly waned, and Devil's Den didn't even make it off the ground. I was concerned that the field information about Devil's Den get back to Florida along with the bones. So far I haven't been able to find any field notes here so I hope that means they were sent to Florida with the bones. The bottom line is that the skeletal remains from Devil's Den remain unstudied—a nice project for someone in Florida.

The human skeletal remains from Devil's Den were returned to the Florida Museum of Natural History in the summer of 2003. Since Devil's Den, Vero, Melbourne, and Warm Mineral Springs are, so far, the only sites in Florida where human skeletal remains appear to be associated with extinct fauna, I immediately began seeking assistance from a biological anthropologist in the Department of Anthropology at the University of Florida to describe the anatomical features of the bones, determine the minimum number of individuals, and access whether they might be datable by radiocarbon analysis. From August 2003 until the spring of 2005, I was kept on hold about this project. In early 2005, I had occasion to contact Dr. Thomas W. Stafford Jr., a well-respected stratigrapher and geochemist, about another matter. He has been instrumental in furnishing precise radiocarbon assessments for bone from ancient archaeological sites and is also attempting to apply innovative dating techniques to fossilized bone in cases where the organic fraction is missing; i.e., he is experimenting with dating inorganic fractions of bone (bone apatite). Dr. Stafford visited Florida for a week in June 2005 and, along with other activities, studied the Devil's Den human bones and concluded there were several individuals represented by crania and postcranial fragments. A brief summary of his work will be discussed in the section about possible twenty-first-century technology and expertise that could be utilized to shed light on the enduring mystery of Florida's first people.

No archaeological investigations of Devil's Den have been conducted since the early 1960s. However, on December 11, 1991, Michael E. Stallings returned human and animal bones to the sink that had been recovered by a diver earlier in the month. The human remains consisted of a radius, two molars, and the parietal portion of a skull.

Silver Springs

Silver Springs is a collective term for at least twelve springs in Marion County located approximately six miles northeast of Ocala. The Silver Springs Group, flowing from numerous vents, forms the headwaters of the Silver River, a tributary of the Oklawaha River, which is a major tributary of the St. Johns River. The main spring or headspring of the Silver River (Mammoth Spring) is a 1st magnitude spring and the largest single-vent artesian spring in the world (see Fig. 2.6). The spring pool measures 300 feet (91.4 meters) north to south and 195 feet (59.4 meters) east to west with a depth of 33 feet (10.1 meters). An underwater cave system has been mapped at the main spring (Fig. 2.10). The west side of the pool was developed into a dock for the famous glass-bottom boats of the Silver Springs theme park (Scott et al. 2004: 244).

From the floor of the headspring in 1949, divers brought up great numbers of animal bones, especially mastodon and mammoth but also saber-toothed tigers, camels, bison, horses, and wolves. Later, in 1953, when an underwater cavern approximately 35 feet below the surface of the water was explored, abundant bones of several extinct species were recovered from the floor of the cavern which extended 45 feet back from its mouth.

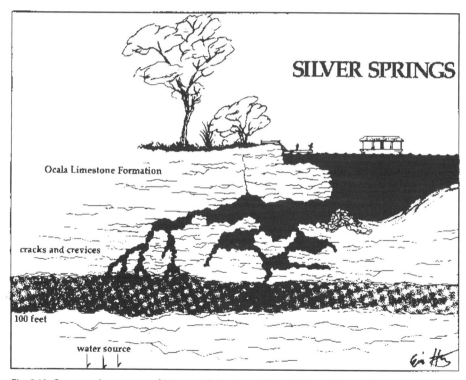

Fig. 2.10. Caves and passages of Mammoth Spring at Silver Springs, Marion County, mapped by Eric Hutcheson in 1993 (courtesy of Silver Springs Nature's Theme Park). Since Eric Hutcheson drew this map, his team of explorers delved deeper into the spring and discovered additional caves and paassages in the search for Mammoth's water source.

Subsequent diving in the cavern brought up a fragment of human skull and the base of what appears to be a Suwannee point. Neill (1964: 26–29) determined that if the water table dropped by no more than 45 feet, the cavern would be a dry and roomy cave and "at the cavern mouth there would be a small ledge on which one could sit and look out over the springhead basin." In 1960, assisted by a local diver, he searched for objects that might have remained in situ in the sand of the ledge. He recovered a Suwannee-like point, several utilized and nonutilized flint flakes, a fragment of mastodon tooth, the tooth of a large horse, and a thin sheet of elephant ivory. He concluded that "the material from the ledge is attributable to Suwannee occupation of the cavern at a time when the water table was much lower than at present, and that subsequent rise of the water table did not significantly disturb the position of these objects. The cavern and ledge are thought to constitute a 'site' in the archaeological sense, hereafter called the Cavern Site [8MR59]" (Neill 1964:29).

In 1952–1953 and periodically until 1955, Wilfred Neill excavated 11 test squares at Paradise Park located on a wooded hill half a mile below the headspring on the south side of Silver Springs Run. The hill is composed of windblown dune sand, part of which had been removed with hand shovels for use elsewhere. From time to time, artifacts were found in the removed sand, including Clovis-like projectile points as well as more recent stone and ceramic materials. Neill (1958: 33–52) hoped to find stratified occupation levels by excavating on the cut face of the sand hill. The sand is about 89–97 inches deep in the area of the test squares and rests on a laminated formation of alternating sand and reddish clay (see his Plate 5, p. 51). The hill drops off to the river on the north, and a small chert quarry is located south of the hill. Beginning at 7 inches below surface to a depth of 93 inches, Neill recovered ceramic and stone artifacts of nearly all known prehistoric time periods in temporally correct position within the deposit. He describes the cultural material level by level moving back into time. Approximately a foot of nearly sterile sand occurred from 74 to 87 inches below surface. Clovis points were encountered from 88 to 93 inches below surface (1–4 inches above the top laminated sand/clay layer). No bone material survived at Paradise Park, but the stratified position of the Suwannee points is significant and can be compared to other sites in Florida with similar strata and artifacts.

Twenty years later, in 1973, E. Thomas Hemmings conducted investigations at the Silver Springs site (8MR92) located in the area of Paradise Park to verify and clarify Neill's observations (Hemmings 1975). He excavated along the face of the old sand borrow pit in the vicinity of Neill's tests. From his excavations and from additional reconnaissance along the Silver Springs Run, Hemmings identified and described six depositional units. Units A_1 through A_4 are Late Pleistocene and Recent, B is clay which Hemmings says is Hawthorne dating to the Plio-Pleistocene, and C is Ocala limestone of Eocene age. Unit A_1 is eolian sand with a maximum thickness of 8.5 feet. A_2 is sand or clayey sand with seepage lines called "laminations" by Neill. It is 7 feet thick, partly wind blown and partly slope wash. The seepage lines are postdepositional effects of groundwater. A_3 is peaty muck of more recent age. A_4 is shelly marl, 12 feet or more thick (Figs. 2.11 and 2.12). Hemmings essentially verified Neill's cultural sequence but found only two in situ flakes and no diagnostic tools in the Paleoindian level at 8.5 feet.

Around 1970, Mr. George William Guest discovered bones eroding from the south bank of Silver Springs Run, 3 meters below the surface of the water, several kilometers east and downstream from the main boil of Silver Springs (Hoffman 1983: 83). Guest went to Benjamin Waller with some of the bones and traded them and information about the location of the site for antique bottles (Waller 1983: 33). Waller visited the site and found preserved mammoth jaws and two bone pins. The bones were lying beneath 1–2 meters of interbedded muck and marl sediments in a matrix of finely crushed shell (the shelly marl described by Hemmings 1975). In 1973, Charles A. Hoffman of Northern Arizona University initiated a four-year formal archaeological investigation at the Guest site (8MR130). He describes (1983: 83–87) the excavation techniques utilized. By the end of the first field season in January 1973, the remains of at least three mammoths, fragments of bison, large cat, deer, turtle, and alligator had been uncovered (Fig. 2.13). The only evidence of human presence was a large quantity of tiny thinning chert flakes found in the rib area of one mam-

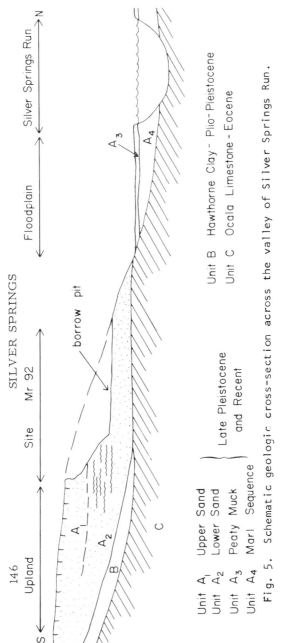

Fig. 5. Schematic geologic cross-section across the valley of Silver Springs Run.

Fig. 2.11. Schematic geologic cross-section across the valley of Silver Springs Run (from Hemmings 1975; courtesy of the Florida Museum of Natural History).

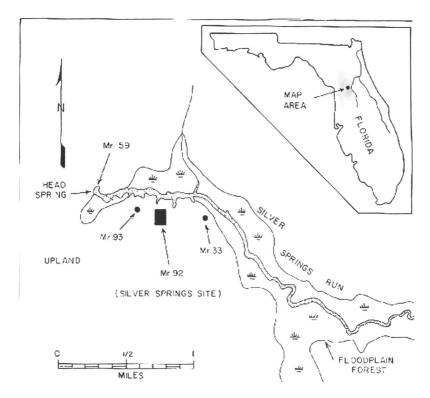

Fig. 2.12. Upper valley of Silver Springs Run showing locations of the headspring, channel, floodplain, upland terrain, and selected archaeological sites (from Hemmings 1975; courtesy of the Florida Museum of Natural History).

moth. But in the summer of 1973, by going deeper into the crushed shell stratum, Hoffman found artifactual material along with more mammoth bone. Ten to 12 feet below modern spring level, a small stemless, lozenge-shaped point was recovered in the vicinity of the proximal end of the right femur close to the ilium of a juvenile Columbian mammoth (Fig. 2.14); chert flakes were found in the area of the ribs and vertebra. Gakushuin University in Tokyo, Japan, radiocarbon-dated collagen of a mammoth bone at 9840±190 (GaK-4512), but this date is not considered accurate. Rayl (1974) furnishes a detailed study of the result of the fieldwork.

Fig. 2.13. Bones of elephants as exposed at the Guest Mammoth site (from Hoffman 1983: 86).

Archaeological interest in Silver Springs dates at least to 1895 with Clarence B. Moore and continues to this day. But Silver Springs is more than just a place to dig up Native American artifacts. It has been an attraction of great beauty and life-giving resources for thousands of years. Richard A. Martin (1966) describes Silver Springs as "A Quiet Miracle," including, from ancient to modern times, the geology, prehistoric inhabitants, Seminoles, first white settlers, the Steamboat Era, famous early tourists, glass-bottom boats, Tarzan movies, and more. Let us hope it remains an "Eternal Spring."

Fig. 2.14. A Paleoindian lanceolate point found between the upper right femur and the pelvis of a mammoth at the Guest Mammoth site (from Hoffman 1983: 87).

Warm Mineral Springs

Warm Mineral Springs (8SO19) is a 3rd magnitude spring located in the town of North Port, Sarasota County. It measures 252 feet (76.8 meters) north to south and 315 feet (96 meters) east to west. A small spring run exits on the west side and flows southwest into the Myakka River. The bottom of the pool slopes gently to a depth of 17 feet (5.2 meters) at about 40 feet (12.2 meters) from shore, where it drops off through a circular opening about 150 feet (46 meters) in diameter to 230 feet (70 meters) below surface. There is a debris cone about 100 feet (30.5 meters) above the deepest part of the bottom (Scott et al. 2004: 265) (Fig. 2.15a, b). It is the only warm mineral spring in the state of Florida and has an average year-round temperature of 87°F. Warm Mineral Springs and the surrounding area was surveyed before the Civil War, but the first description of the spring appears in *Wild Life in Florida* (1875) when the author, F. Trench Townshend, found the spring cloaked by a dense growth of palmetto, acacia, and oak.

No archaeological research has been carried out at Warm Mineral Springs since 1991, and the present owners do not allow any diving (Steve Koski, personal communication, June 17, 2006). Therefore, in the following paragraphs, I will summarize information from Purdy (1991: 178–204), which is an account of investigations at the site from the late 1950s to the termination of excavations.

People had been swimming in the spring for generations, but no one had dived deep into its abyss until Lieutenant Colonel William R. Royal retired from the Air Force and returned to Florida. Although Royal had been free diving up to 40 or 50 feet for years, he began using scuba equipment as soon as it became available. On November 26, 1958, he dove in Warm Mineral Springs for the first time and discovered stalactites (dripstones) at 25 and ca. 60 feet, indicating that the water level in the spring had been much lower because stalactites form only in dry caves (Fig. 2.16). On his descent into the spring he also noticed a ledge at 45 feet (13 meters) covered with loose black sediments up to 4 feet thick. That same evening, he wrote letters to various university geology departments in the state describing his discovery and asking for help in verifying his interpretation. H. K. Brooks, a geologist and diver at the University of Florida, responded to Royal's request but did not immediately confirm Royal's observation, saying "science does not lend itself to sensationalism" (Royal 1978: 146). John M. Goggin, the only scuba-diving archaeologist in America at the time, visited both Little Salt Spring and Warm Mineral Springs with his students and also reacted negatively to Royal's overenthusiasm (Goggin 1960, 1962). But Royal could not wait to announce his discoveries to the world, and, after considerable press coverage, arrangements were made with Chet Huntley of the National Broadcasting Company to film a special report on the springs and Royal's discoveries which, by this time, in-

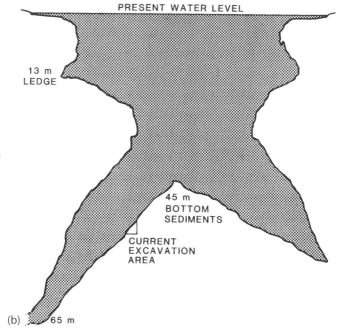

Fig. 2.15. (a) Air view of Warm Mineral Springs; (b) cross-sectional view of Warm Mineral Springs showing the present water level, the 45-foot (13 meter) ledge, and the location of excavations in the bottom sediments at 200 feet (not to scale) (from Purdy 1991).

PRESENT WATER LEVEL

13 m
LEDGE

45 m
BOTTOM
SEDIMENTS

CURRENT
EXCAVATION
AREA

(b)   65 m

Fig. 2.16. Stalactites in Warm Mineral Springs (courtesy of William R. Royal).

cluded human bones. On July 11, 1959, the cameras caught Royal surfacing at Warm Mineral Springs with a skull in his hands and portions of brain material dribbling from the cranium (Fig. 2.17). (See also Royal and Clark 1960.) After this scene was witnessed nationwide on the Huntley-Brinkley news show, the spring was visited by divers who ravaged large portions of the stratified deposits on the 45-foot (13-meter) ledge.

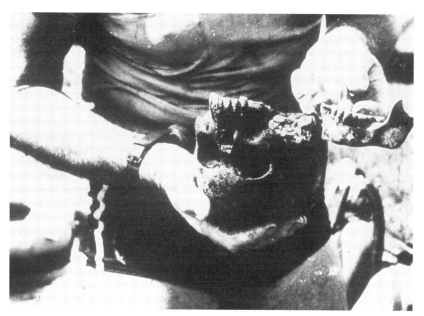

Fig. 2.17. William R. Royal looking at brain tissue through the foramen magnum of the Royal skull immediately after it was recovered from the 13-meter ledge in 1959 (courtesy of William R. Royal).

Fortunately, H. K. Brooks had spent considerable time mapping, photographing, and collecting carefully zoned samples of the sediments in the spring for faunal, floral, petrographic, and radiometric analyses, including those on the 45-foot ledge. He identified three zones on the ledge: from top to bottom, Zone 1, 20–50 centimeters thick, was a black algal ooze with shells of small snails and occasional bones of alligator, tarpon, and turtle; Zone 2, 15–50 centimeters thick, was unconsolidated gray calcitic mud with snail shells, pine bark, oak leaves, other plant debris, and bones of frogs and mice; Zone 3, 10–80 centimeters thick, was a leaf bed with alternating strata of calcitic mud containing terrestrial and freshwater snails. Vertebrate remains in Zone 3 were identified as human, deer, opossum, raccoon, rabbit, squirrel, mouse, and frog. Radiocarbon dates for Zone 2 were ca. 8500±400 years and ca. 9000–10,500 for numerous samples from Zone 3.

Zones 1 and 2 had been largely destroyed, and Zone 3 sediments had undergone extensive damage by January 1972 when Carl J. Clausen excavated a small but controlled test in an area on the 45-foot ledge where Zone 3 was undisturbed. The 1-x-5-meter test unit represents the first time that a controlled archaeological excavation was undertaken in this type of finely stratified deposit under water. The procedures are described explicitly and are well documented with underwater photographs in Clausen et al. (1975a, b). No artifacts were found, but in Level 4 (30–40 centimeters) of Zone 3, a first sacral vertebra of a human juvenile was discovered. Associated botanical materials were dated by radiocarbon analysis at ca. 10,000 B.P. These are the first and earliest human bones recoverd under completely documented and controlled systematic excavations in the Southeast. Earlier, while preparing the unit to expose the stratigraphy, Clausen recovered a fragmentary left ilium of a human juvenile; both bones are thought to belong to the same six-year-old child.

The 45-foot (13-meter) ledge at Warm Mineral Springs was the primary location of discoveries, collecting, systematic excavations, and controversy. William R. Royal removed most of the human bones from the 13-meter ledge, including 7 skulls (6 adults and 1 child) and other skeletal material representing 30 individuals. One of the skulls, the White Skull, came from a grey-green clay stratum below Zone 3. On February 5, 1973, Wilburn A. Cockrell recovered a fairly complete skeleton of an adult male from the ledge at the base of Zone 3 which was radiocarbon-dated at nearly 10,000 years old (Fig. 2.18). The recovery of this individual, Warm Mineral Springs Man, received extensive and sensationalized attention in the popular media. Subsequently, Cockrell and Murphy (1978) recovered sabre-tooth cat, ground sloth, panther, deer, opossum, raccoon, frog, turtle, and an edentulous human mandible from the grey-green clay stratum, which dated to 10,980±40 B.P.

Donald H. Morris (1975) determined that Warm Mineral Springs Man and the White Skull along with the edentulous mandible represented the earliest aboriginal human inhabitants of Florida and suggested that they may be contemporaneous with the Vero and Melbourne finds of several decades earlier. Morris concluded that Warm Mineral Springs Man was a slender adult, somewhat short for Indians north of Mexico (5 feet, 4 inches), who died in his fourth decade. The mandible may belong to the

Recovered parts are solid.

BURIAL NO. 1   8So19

SKELETAL ELEMENTS PRESENT

Fig. 2.18. Warm Mineral Springs Man (courtesy of Donald H. Morris and the Florida Museum of Natural History).

White Skull because the size is compatible; if so, the White Skull is probably that of an older woman.

Cockrell and Murphy's work at Warm Mineral Springs throughout the rest of the 1970s and 1980s consisted of additional mapping, three-dimensional gridding, and excavations, which were recorded on videotape using a special underwater camera and light source. Excellent studies of the fauna (McDonald 1975) and flora (King 1975; Sheldon and Cameron 1976) were conducted at Warm Mineral Springs. McDonald identified the following different types of vertebrate animals: 6 fish, 4 amphibians, 12 reptiles, 11 birds, and 22 mammals, including at least 4 extinct species from the grey-green clay zone. The pollen and plant remains from 9000–10,000 years B.P. at Warm Mineral Springs indicate a mixed hardwood forest of mesic species, which are adapted to moderately wet habitats. The artifacts from the 45-foot ledge are meagre. Royal collected two stone points called Green Briar (similar to Bolen), and Cockrell recovered what appears to be an atlatl spur of carved shell when he removed Warm Mineral Springs Man in 1973.

William R. Royal did not pretend to be an archaeologist, but it is lamentable that his methods of retrieval and subsequent displaying of his finds—cementing them into his fireplace—have made it impossible to document convincingly the significance of the materials from the 45-foot ledge at Warm Mineral Springs (Fig. 2.19). On the other hand, if Dr. John M. Goggin had been more patient with Royal's ignorance of archaeological techniques and goals, he would not have turned his back on one of the most important ancient finds in the Western Hemisphere. For more detail, see Goggin (1960, 1962), Royal (1978), and Purdy (1991).

Disagreement arose between Carl J. Clausen and Wilburn A. Cockrell about whether the deposits on the 45-foot ledge were laid down in subaqueous or dry conditions. It seems obvious that in order for the organic materials to survive, particularly the flora, they had to remain constantly wet, indicating that the water in the spring was at the level of the 45-foot ledge or higher when deposition of Zone 3 occurred about 10,000 years B.P. There is actually no real controversy because Clausen and Cockrell excavated in different areas of the ledge, and Clausen apparently did not penetrate the grey-green clay below Zone 3. Cockrell and Murphy, on the other hand, found bones with teeth marks indicating that the ledge was dry when the edentulous mandible and extinct animals were deposited there. I think the grey-green stratum should have been labeled Zone 4.

Clausen et al. (1975a: 212) believed that material antedating that found on the 45-foot ledge would be present in the debris cone at the bottom of the spring. In the mid-1980s, Cockrell began excavations in the debris cone at 155 feet (ca. 48 meters) (Fig. 2.15b). The first few inches of the unit produced a 1930s Coca-Cola bottle and a 78-rpm phonograph record. Most of the finds were alligator coprolites (Skow 1986). The work was

Fig. 2.19. William R. Royal displaying his fireplace and some of the materials recovered from Warm Mineral Springs and Little Salt Spring (courtesy of William R. Royal).

discontinued for two years because of a diving accident and had just resumed when I visited the site in early 1990. Cockrell estimated that he had reached a 3,000-year level. With limited bottom time at that depth (155 feet), systematic excavations are slow and difficult. A decision was made in 1991 to cease archaeological excavations at Warm Mineral Springs because nothing of any significance was being added to the information already attained.

In addition to the damage caused by divers after Royal's 1959 television appearance with brain material oozing from a human skull, the spring area has been modified to accommodate bathers. For nearly 50 years sand has been dumped in the shallow water of the spring to provide a wading beach. Some of the sand has drifted into the cavern where it erodes the walls and settles on the 45-foot ledge and debris cone at the bottom. One wonders, therefore, if anything significant is left or accessible on the ledge. It would be interesting to find out if a portion of the grey-green clay is still intact. If so, it might furnish positive proof that humans and extinct animals cohabitated that area of Florida before the end of the Pleistocene.

Little Salt Spring

Little Salt Spring (8SO18) and Warm Mineral Springs are less than 2 miles (3.12 kilometers) apart in the town of North Port, Sarasota County. Little Salt Spring is a basinlike depression 257.4 feet (78 meters) across and 198 feet (60 meters) deep. The floor of the basin slopes at 25° from the land surface to 39.6 feet (12 meters) in depth where it drops off (Fig. 2.20). The center of the depression is a circular opening 82.5–99 feet (25–30 meters) across (Clausen et al. 1979: 609) (Fig. 2.21). Several water sources or vents have been identified on the bottom of the spring at 264 feet (80 meters) below surface (Gomez and Coy 2006). A freshwater cenote existed at Little Salt Spring when semiarid conditions prevailed in Florida 12,000–13,500 years ago. The water level in the spring was 90 feet (27 meters) lower at that time, and its xerophytic surroundings lacked abundant flowing surface water. Because of lowered sea level, the site was much farther from the Gulf Coast than it is today.

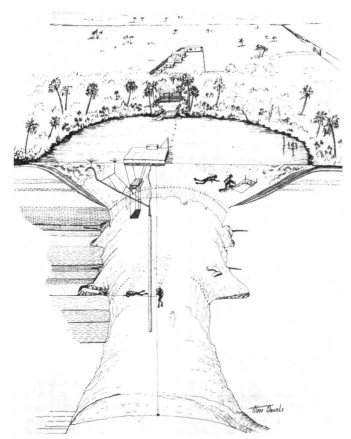

Fig. 2.20. Little Salt Spring showing 16-meter ledge, 27-meter ledge, the slope of the basin, and the debris cone at the bottom of the spring (courtesy of William R. Royal).

In early 1959, when Lieutenant Colonel William R. Royal first heard about Little Salt Spring, it was located on property belonging to the Mackle Brothers Land Developing Company. It took Royal three days to find the spring: "It was in open prairie country but hidden in the heart of a jungle hammock so thick it was difficult to worm our way in carrying our diving gear. When we broke through the vegetation and saw that quiet round pool of dark water several hundred feet across, we were sweaty and tired but elated" (Royal 1978: 142). The spring and vicinity are still pristine

Fig. 2.21. Little Salt Spring from the air (courtesy of John A. Gifford).

today, but the surrounding land has been extensively developed; it is no longer a "jungle."

Royal found and removed large numbers of human bones from the slough and basin area of Little Salt Spring (Fig. 2.22). When John M. Goggin arrived in Northport with his students, Royal took them to the spring: "It was my impression that this was supposed to be a scientifically controlled dive, but to my amazement Dr. Goggin let his students run rampant in the spring. . . . they came to the surface with their pockets, shirts, hands and arms full of bones . . . they looked like grave robbers on a spree. All the finds were dumped into our small boat until the bottom of it was deep in human bones" (Royal 1978:150).

Shortly, Mackle Brothers closed Little Salt Spring to divers unless they signed a waiver that released Mackle Brothers from responsibility in event of diver injury or fatality. Soon thereafter, they closed the spring to diving entirely. Royal had permission to dive if he walked into the site. Finally,

Fig. 2.22. William R. Royal in the late 1950s with human skeletal material and artifacts at Little Salt Spring (courtesy of William R. Royal).

John Goggin prevailed upon Mackle Brothers to close the spring altogether to divers.

Mackle Brothers became General Development Corporation in the 1960s and created a General Development Foundation that funded most of the research at Little Salt Spring during the 1970s. The foundation was dissolved in 1980, and General Development Corporation deeded Little Salt Spring and the 110-acre buffer over to the University of Miami on April 13, 1982 (John Gifford, personal communication, 2006).

The slough and basin were identified as an Archaic Period cemetery dating to approximately 5,200 to 6,800 years old. Hundreds of deceased individuals were interred in the moist soft peat of the slough accompanied by all manner of grave goods that furnished important information about lifestyles of that time. As at similarly dated water-saturated sites in Florida, human brain matter survived in a number of crania in the cemetery at Little Salt Spring. One cannot help but wonder if it might have been a skull from this slough that Royal held in front of the cameras at Warm Mineral Springs on July 11, 1959, since brain material has not been found in any of the other human remains from Warm Mineral Springs. Farther down the slope toward the drop-off, Early Archaic or Late Paleoindian cultural materials along with all modern fauna have been recovered dating to 9,000–10,000 years old (Clausen et al. 1979). Research is still ongoing in this area (Gifford 2006; Koski 2006), and very significant finds are being made. In addition, on a recent reconnaissance dive to the 16-meter ledge, two localities were recorded that are wide enough to put in test pits (Gifford, personal communication, 2006) (See Fig. 2.20). This ledge was not excavated in the 1970s and may contain important archaeological and environmental information.

The 90-foot (27-meter) ledge is the location of interest in this volume. Unfortunately, no excavations of the ledge have been conducted since the 1970s when Carl J. Clausen (Clausen et al. 1979) found the overturned, collapsed shell of an extinct species of giant land tortoise with a sharply pointed wooden stake between the carapace and plastron (Fig. 2.23a, b). Wood from the stake was dated by carbon 14 at 12,030 years ago, and the carbonate fraction of a tortoise bone was dated at 13,450 years ago. Several bones appeared carbonized, and numerous fragments of fire-hardened

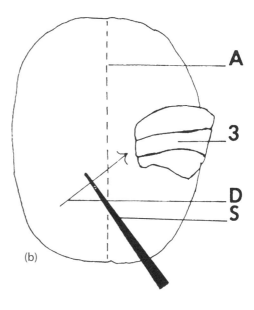

(b)

(a)

Fig. 2.23. (a) Wooden stake and (b) diagram showing its association with the giant land tortoise (*Geochelone crassiscutata*) (courtesy of John A. Gifford).

clay were found under and around the animal's remains. Apparently, the tortoise was killed and possibly cooked in an upside-down position. In addition to the tortoise, other extinct species identified from the 27-meter ledge include three smaller tortoises of the same species, a large box turtle, ground sloth, and portions of an immature mastodon. Several extant species were also recovered (Holman and Clausen 1984). No human remains have been reported so far from this ledge at Little Salt Spring.

Renewed investigations of the 27-meter ledge are planned. The overburden of organic detritus needs to be cleared from the ledge in order to expose the underlying clay and rock deposits. When this task is completed, excavations can be carried out to prove or disprove that the clay stratum of the ledge contains human remains associated with now-extinct faunal species (John A. Gifford, personal communication, 2006).

In 1990, John A. Gifford received funds from the National Geographic Society (Grant 4217–89) to conduct a paleoenvironmental study of the debris deposit that lies 60 meters below surface at Little Salt Spring. By vibracoring below the sediment-water interface, Gifford hoped to procure samples for radiocarbon dating and microfossil analysis that would furnish information about climate and vegetation dating perhaps to the full glacial period about 18,000 or more years ago. He obtained a total of eight cores, six of which were kept (Fig. 2.24). At 11 meters below the sediment-water interface in a sandy matrix containing gravel, pebbles, and occasional mammal bones, radiocarbon analysis on a wood sample returned a date of 12,210±190 (calibrated 13,820–14,447, Beta-42294) (Fig. 2.25). For greater detail and significance of the 1990 coring project at Little Salt Spring, see Zarikian et al. (2005: 134–156).

See Purdy (1991: 139–158 and references) for additional information about Little Salt Spring.

Rivers

For many years, divers and hobbyists have collected all manner of bones and artifacts while exploring Florida's shallow riverbeds. These objects afford a potentially valuable view of the ancient and not so ancient past, but their value is diminished because they were not recovered in strati-

Fig. 2.24. Portions of three 10-foot sections of a 40-foot (12-meter) core from Little Salt Spring showing organic sediments and laminations (courtesy of John A. Gifford).

fied deposits and cannot be dated; in addition, divers and hobbyists do not always record geographic locations and associated materials. If, however, the artifacts are stylistically similar to those from other areas, and if modified bones belong to animals that have been extinct for thousands of years, the specimens alone are important additions to the database. Paleoindian artifacts and extinct Pleistocene megafauna have been found in the Chipola, Withlacoochee, Wacissa, Aucilla, Santa Fe, Ichetucknee, Suwannee, Silver, Oklawaha, St. Johns, and other rivers. Objects from some of these rivers have already been discussed. The work conducted in the late twentieth century on the Aucilla deserves special mention.

The Page-Ladson Site (8JE591)

As stated earlier, the discovery of a *Bison antiquus* skull in the Wacissa River with a "spearhead" embedded in the right fronto-parietal area (see Fig. 2.5) served as a catalyst for paleontologists and archaeologists to work

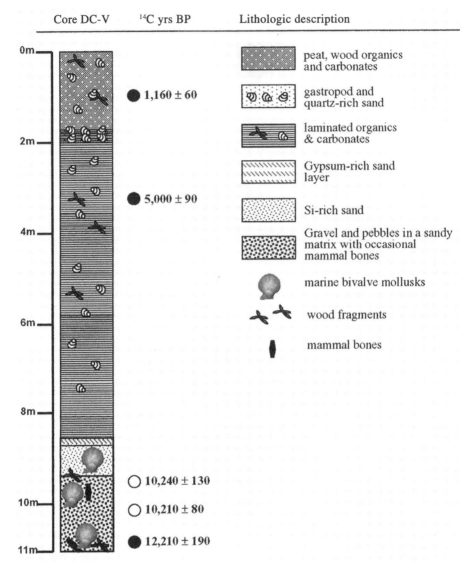

Fig. 2.25. Lithostratigraphy of a Little Salt Spring core. Circles indicate stratigraphic position of AMS radiocarbon-dated wood and charcoal samples (from Zarikian et al. 2005; courtesy of Elsevier Press and John A. Gifford).

more closely together to document the contemporaneity of humans and Late Ice Age fauna. The 11,170±130 RCYBP (Beta 5942) bison was a six- to ten-year-old female. The protruding part of the stone fragment was lenticular in cross section (Webb et al. 1984). The fragment has not been removed or x-rayed (C. Andrew Hemmings, personal communication, 2006). Because of this and other important finds, the Aucilla River Prehistory Project (ARPP) was initiated to recover in situ interactions between the first Floridians and Late Pleistocene megafauna. After nearly 20 years of reconnaissance, excavation, and analysis, the results of the ARPP were compiled into a spectacular volume entitled *First Floridians and Last Mastodons: The Page-Ladson Site on the Aucilla River* (Webb 2006). Also, throughout the years, progress reports and descriptions of interesting discoveries at the site appeared in numerous publications, particularly the *Aucilla River Times*. The ARPP was funded generously by the National Geographic Society and the Florida Division of Historical Resources and supported by the Florida Museum of Natural History and many other contributors. The Florida Museum of Natural History was awarded a number of special category grants, without which the project would not have succeeded. In the following paragraphs, I give a brief summary of the research and its significance.

The Page-Ladson site is located just below the point where its tributary, the Wacissa River, flows into the widest part of Half-Mile Rise on the lower Aucilla River (see Fig. 1.2). Here, the bottom of the Aucilla River consists of a string of semicircular sinkholes connected by short stretches of shallow limestone. A strong positive correlation exists in Florida between the distribution of Paleoindian artifacts and karst topographic features such as sinkholes. These sinkholes were isolated sources of water (cenotes) when sea level was lower during the Late Pleistocene. They gradually filled with colluvial and other deposits of silts, clays, and peats. Excavations were designed to test the hypothesis that these sinkholes were kill site/camp areas and that sediments deposited for thousands of years were in stratigraphic position and datable. Page-Ladson was chosen because it contained an intact column of about 7+ meters of organic-rich sediments from which a score or more of radiocarbon dates were obtained. The sedimentary record corresponds well with sea level rise of the last glacial cycle. The 10,000 RCYBP Bolen surface is the youngest intact human occupation known in the Aucilla.

The nearly continuous sequence from more than 12,000 RCYBP at the Page-Ladson site included a high percentage of peat that preserved a diverse array of organic specimens, such as wood, seeds, pollen, bone, ivory, mollusks, and ostracods. Sophisticated studies of all these materials were conducted and are summarized in Webb (2006). The plants, both pollen and macrophytic remains, clearly reflect a picture of climatic change and environment from the Late Pleistocene into the early Holocene. Extinct fauna identified from Page-Ladson include mammoth, mastodon, tapir, llama, sloth, horse, extinct tortoise, and giant armadillo. Several of the peaty sediments dating 12,600–11,600 RCYBP consist predominantly of *Mammut americanum* digesta, which provide a fascinating window into diet and seasonal patterns of these proboscideans. Strontium isotope data revealed that the mastodons at the Page-Ladson site were migratory and left the coastal plain for granitic terrain, the nearest of which is in central Georgia. A discussion of the artifacts recovered, including modified bones of extinct animals, will be found in the section titled "Paleoindian Artifacts."

The ARPP, under the leadership of James Dunbar, underwater archaeologist, and David Webb, underwater paleontologist, "attracted an extraordinarily talented and dedicated group of amateurs and professionals, who served variously as underwater excavators, equipment operators, fundraisers, conservators, data-managers, and in innumerable other jobs that have no rubrics" (Webb and Hemmings 2001:3). This 20-year project afforded an opportunity to discover evidence of Paleoindians and megafauna in a new environmental and stratigraphic context, i.e., an underwater setting. The interdisplinary approach and the single-focus research design were important components in making this one of the most informative Paleoindian studies ever conducted in Florida.

Other important sites in the Aucilla and Wacissa rivers are Ryan-Harley (8JE1004), Little River Rapids (8JE603), Sloth Hole (8JE121), Fossil Hole (8JE1497), Ohmes Hole (8JE122), and Gingery Cache (8TA99).

St. Johns

Several locations that have not been investigated professionally are re-ported in Lake George near Drayton Island and some drowned springs. Extinct Pleistocene fauna, 50 unfluted Paleoindian points, and hundreds of utilized chert flakes and tools have been recovered (David Thulman, personal communication, 2006).

Stone Quarries and Workshops

In addition to uplands adjacent to springs and spring runs, such as at Hornsby and Silver Springs, there are other stone quarry and workshop sites where Paleoindian points or tools have been found in the lowest cultural stratum. Examples include Bolen Bluff south of Paynes Prairie in Alachua County (Bullen 1958), Johnson's Lake in the northwestern part of Marion County (Bullen and Dolan 1959), and Harney Flats (8HI507) in Hillsborough County (Daniel and Wisenbaker 1987). The deposits at these sites are typically less than a meter deep and tend to be located on bluffs overlooking or close to water sources. They can be dated only by the comparative method because no animals or plants have survived for radiocarbon analysis. Nevertheless, when their data are added to that of other sites already discussed, there is little doubt (1) that Suwannee points and tools underlie the more recent stemmed varieties of the Archaic Pe-riod and (2) that these Suwannee points have been found in other loca-tions in association with extinct Late Pleistocene fauna.

Offshore Sites

Because numerous Paleoindian-style stone tools were recovered from dredged deposits in the Tampa Bay area (Goodyear et al. 1983; Warren 1966, 1968), and because of Ruppé's pioneering work regarding drowned terrestrial sites (Ruppé 1980), it was hypothesized that portions of the Aucilla River now submerged on the continental shelf would contain stratified deposits dating to the Late Pleistocene. A Florida State Univer-sity project was initiated in 1986 and eventually called "PaleoAucilla Pre-history—Clovis Underwater." Test pits at the J&J Hunt site in 1998, located about three miles offshore on the margin of what may be remnants of the Aucilla, produced stone tools and debitage but no diagnostic early points in situ. The area was inundated about 6800 RCYBP (Faught 1999: 5).

While it is logical that offshore sites exist in places where rivers once flowed through now-drowned terrestrial landscapes, the difficulty and expense of reconnaissance and excavation at these locations have hampered recovery of this valuable information. Rosenau et al. (1977) identify many springs offshore on the Atlantic and Gulf coasts of Florida. Considering the popularity of springs throughout time, these locations may be important areas to investigate.

Paleoindian Artifacts

Stone and bone (including ivory) are the only materials from which artifacts were manufactured that have survived from the Late Ice Age of Florida. Diagnostic stone specimens include distinctive types of projectile points made of chert (flint) (see Fig. 2.1), exquisite unifacial tools also made of chert (Fig. 2.26), and, possibly, ground stone objects variously called bola stones, clubheads, egg stones, or dimple stones often produced from nonlocal quartzites, sandstones, and limestones (see Fig. 2.3b). Modified anatomical elements (see Fig. 2.4) and implements manufactured from bones (Fig. 2.27) or tusks (Fig. 2.28a–c) of extinct animal species furnish unquestionable evidence that people and Late Pleistocene fauna coexisted in Florida; thus, they are also diagnostic.

By diagnostic I mean that if objects are found out of context, that is, not recovered from a discrete position in a datable stratigraphic profile, they can still be recognized (1) by their style in the case of stone artifacts or (2) by the fact that they were manufactured or modified from extinct species of Late Pleistocene animals.

Lanceolate Points

Stone spearheads have been referred to in several places throughout this volume. They are beautifully made, perfectly symmetrical stemless specimens with grinding or smoothing of the base and lower lateral edges interpreted as a means to faciliate hafting without cutting the binding

Fig. 2.26. Paleoindian unifacial tools (from Purdy 1981).

Fig. 2.27. Dagger manufactured from metatarsal bone of *Equus* sp. (extinct horse), Lower Aucilla River (photo by William O. Gifford; courtesy of C. Andrew Hemmings).

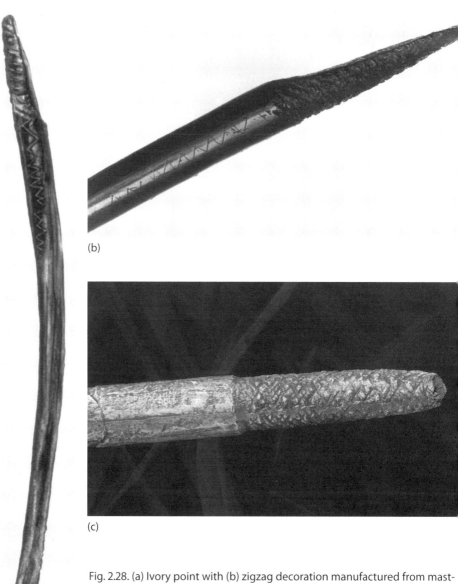

(b)

(c)

(a)

Fig. 2.28. (a) Ivory point with (b) zigzag decoration manufactured from mastodon tusk (courtesy of S. David Webb and the Florida Museum of Natural History); (c) close-up of hatching on an ivory point (photo by Scott Mitchum; courtesy of the Silver River Museum).

material. Fluting—the removal of one or more flakes from the base—is often present but does not *have* to be a characteristic to classify a point as Paleoindian. There is some disagreement about the contemporaneity of Clovis, Suwannee, and Simpson points in Florida. As a matter of fact, there are very few sites throughout the country where one type of Paleoindian point occurs below another type in secure enough stratigraphic position with supporting dates and accompanying data to draw definitive conclusions about antiquity. An exception to this statement is the superposition of Folsom to Clovis from at least one site in western North America. As a result, this may have created a problem because the assumption has been made that Clovis always occupies the lowest rung on the Paleoindian ladder. There have been enough locations in Florida where Suwannee points are found in fairly well documented association with extinct animals to conclude that these points were being made when some Pleistocene megafauna still roamed the state. Just because Folsom is younger than Clovis in the West, does this mean that Suwannee is younger than Clovis in Florida? At present, this is a moot question because there is no evidence.

A topic already addressed by others (Dunbar and Hemmings 2004; Edwards 1954; Neill 1958, 1964; David Thulman, personal communication, 2006) warrants a brief mention here. That is, how different is Clovis typologically from Suwannee and Simpson? Classification systems in general are somewhat subjective. They are based on the image of a particular object or event that is then portrayed in an ideal rendition. All "ideals" deviate in one or more features. If all Florida Paleoindian lanceolate points were placed side by side and an attempt made to classify them as Clovis, Suwannee, or Simpson, it would be apparent that there is a tremendous range of variation within each type and that one point would grade into another at the borders.

Classification is imposed on objects by the classifier and often has little to do with what the maker of an object had in mind 12,000 or more years ago. There are many variables to consider such as regional differences in point manufacture, the quality of stone available, the skill of the flint-knapper, the animal or person that was the intended victim, and probably much more. One important factor is that these people were nomadic. We know that because they had a lightweight, portable tool kit with some items manufactured from non-Florida materials. Several different groups of people may have been visiting Florida seasonally as "snowbirds" or other tourists do today. We know from data at the Page-Ladson site that mastodons migrated into and out of the state; they may have been followed by nomadic hunters. Clovis, Suwannee, and Simpson are all made from a similar blueprint, but every flake is not removed exactly the same way and the final shape does not always conform to the "ideal." Nevertheless, they are collectively more alike than their descendants.

I said that Suwannee points date to the Middle Paleoindian period when "there is some indication that only modern fauna survived in Florida" (Purdy 1996: 7). I now wish to retract that statement. I believe that Suwannee points were associated with still extant Pleistocene fauna.

Unifacial Stone Tools

The following information is taken from Purdy (1996: 10–11). In addition to the distinctive spearhead styles described above, the rest of the Paleoindian tool kit is also unique. It consists of carefully made unifacial blades, knives, scrapers, and other objects of various sizes, shapes, and areas of use (Fig. 2.26). These implements are small and lightweight, reflecting a nomadic existence in which a portable, flexible tool kit was essential. For many years in North America this distinctive tool kit has been recognized as being associated with the Paleoindian period or a big game hunting way of life. Blade tools in particular are considered the hallmark of the Paleoindian period.

These kinds of stone tools are found in rivers and springs in Florida, but it was not until the Harney Flats site was excavated (Daniel and Wisenbaker 1987) that they were found along with Suwannee and Simpson points in a well-documented stratigraphic sequence. The "discovery" of the unpublished dissertation of William Ellis Edwards (1954: 66–68), with a photograph of a group of these unifacial tools that were recovered along with or underlying Suwannee-style lanceolates at the Helen Blazes site, provides another location where these artifacts are associated with Paleoindian-style points in situ. They are described as snub-nosed end scrapers, side scrapers, gravers, etc. Unfortunately, the stone tools and weapons excavated by Edwards seem to have disappeared and the quality of his photographs is poor; his descriptions of the artifacts, however, are very clear.

Another bit of convincing evidence that these nicely made unifacial tools date to the Paleoindian period comes from a lithic quarry site (Purdy 1975) where thousands of Early to Middle Archaic stone implements (ca. 5,000–10,000 years ago) were manufactured. None of them resembled the classic unifacial styles.

It is interesting to note also that many of these tools look exactly like types that were made in various areas of the Old World during the time period known as the Upper Paleolithic.

Ground Stone

What do you call an object of no proven function that is shaped like an egg? Various authors, including this one, called them "bolas," assuming they were tied with thongs, knotted at the indentation, and thrown in groups of three to ensnare the legs of running animals or the wings of birds (Purdy 1981a: 30). Others have called them "clubheads" that were hafted and used as clubs or pounders. The preferred name now seems to be "dimple stone" because it does not imply function but describes the dimple on the proximal end, which is the most characteristic feature of the artifact. Dimple stones are an enigma because they are the only manufactured ground stone artifact dating to the Paleoindian period.

Most Florida specimens were found in and near rivers and were first mentioned by J. Clarence Simpson (1948). Neill (1971) describes a dimple stone from the Cavern site beneath the waters of Silver Springs, which he concluded was from a Paleoindian context. However, only one dimple stone from one archaeological site, Page-Ladson (8JE591), has come from a well-controlled excavation unit of Late Pleistocene age (Dunbar 1996; Rachels and Knight 2004: 61; Tesar 1994: 296). Tesar and Rachels and Knight analyzed some of Florida's dimple stones, including postulated functions, sizes, and locations where recovered, and both cite an unpublished paper by Philip R. Gerrell.

The fact that dimple stones, like unifacial tools, have not been found at excavated sites of Archaic or more recent time periods supports the conclusion reached by Simpson (1948), Neill (1971), and others that they belong to the assemblage of Paleoindian artifacts. Since a majority of these items appear to be made of nonlocal stone, an interesting research project would be an attempt to identify the sources of the stone. With this information, it might be possible to trace the migration routes of some Paleoindian groups.

Bone and Ivory

A thorough study of surviving evidence pertaining to the human use of extinct taxa has been assembled, analyzed, and interpreted by Hemmings (2004). Unless otherwise noted, the following information comes from his dissertation.

There have been 142 ivory tools and 16 modified anatomical elements or tools of bone from extinct species recorded in Florida since the first specimens were recovered in 1927 (Jenks and Simpson 1941). These figures exclude the still controversial objects reported earlier by Sellards at Vero and by Loomis and Gidley at the Melbourne sites. Mammoth (*Mammuthus columbi*), mastodon (*Mammut americanum*), horse (*Equus* sp.), tapir (*Tapirus veroensis*), ground sloth (*Megalonyx jeffersoni*), camel (*Hemiauchehnia macrocephala*), camelops (*Paleolama mirifica*), tortoise (*Geochelone crassiscutata*), bison (*Bison antiquus*), and canis (*Canis dirus?*) are the animals recovered either in submerged archaeological sites or from other locations that show unmistakable modification. The uncertainty about the canis specimen, possibly dire wolf, is that it was not found in context, and it is difficult to distinguish it from *Canis lupus*, a modern but usually smaller animal. See illustration and description of this mandible ornament in Hemmings (2004) and Webb and Hemmings (2001: 6–7). Human modifications of these species range from extremely well made artifacts such as daggers of horse or camel metatarsals (Fig. 2.27) to simple cut marks (Fig. 2.4), calcined areas, or points embedded in a bone such as the bison already discussed (Fig. 2.5) (Webb et al. 1984). The list also includes the knee bone (patella) of an elephant used as an anvil and several atlatl hooks. Many other extinct animal species are found—giant armadillo, bear, sabre cat, peccary, capybara—but do not appear to have been used. Hemmings (2004: 15) observes that when a bone is found with cut marks (butchering?), it was unintended and should occur infrequently. Thousands of artifacts made of fossilized deer bone are recovered, but they probably date to the Holocene.

Ivory artifacts manufactured from extinct elephant tusks are more numerous in Florida than any other location in the Western Hemisphere. Hemmings describes 13 forms of ivory objects including bead preforms, a socketed handle fragment, atlatl hooks, a needle, a barbed point, and the well-known ivory shafts, as well as a graver spur from a mastodon tooth. There are 48 sites in 10 Florida counties where ivory objects have been found. Hemmings believes that Sloth Hole (8JE121) was an ivory industrial site. More than 6,000 fragments and 33 shaft tools were recovered there. Because of the large sample, he was able to study manufacturing techniques and concluded, among other observations, that grinding was a common part of the process.

The ivory shafts made of elephant tusk (principally mastodon) are a long cylinder tapered to a polished point at one end and bevelled and incised with cross-hatching at the thicker end. They were made by cutting and husking the outer ivory lamellae in four segments around and two segments along a fresh tusk core of a mature animal. Only fresh (or frozen) ivory can be worked without shattering. If dried or fossilized, it becomes brittle and delaminates (Dunbar and Webb 1996; Webb et al. 1990).

These weapons were designed to deliver a powerful blow with deep penetration. There are two theories about how they functioned to deliver this blow. The earlier version concluded that they were foreshafts and that a Clovis point was hafted to the bevelled end while the pointed, tapered end was inserted into a socket of a long spear or atlatl. Hemmings (2004: 195) concluded that these artifacts were points, not foreshafts. He furnishes convincing evidence that the pointed, tapered end functioned to penetrate the animal.

The ivory shafts are similar in size and workmanship to examples from other parts of the country. But more significantly, they are the single most important artifact uniting Paleoindian cultures of the Western Hemisphere to Upper Paleolithic cultures of the Old World. Not only are the specimens from both areas nearly identical, but zigzag designs on two of the objects from Florida match similar designs on their Upper Paleolithic counterparts. It is not known if these zigzag lines have practical or spiritual meaning, but they are the earliest indication of artistic expression in the New World (Fig. 2.28).

Conclusion

There is only one conclusion to reach from the evidence cited above. People were in Florida during the Last Ice Age. Even Aleš Hrdlička would have to agree. Human presence has been documented almost statewide and suggests that there was a fairly large population of permanent residents as well as migratory visitors. Thousands of diagnostic Paleoindian stone artifacts and other objects of durable materials have been collected from springs, sinks, rivers, and terrestrial sites. It is reasonable to assume that these surviving items were exceeded tenfold by articles of material culture that perished, such as shelters, clothing, wood, ornaments, weaving, food preparation equipment, and food preferences other than large animals.

Unfortunately, we will never know very much about the people themselves, such as how they raised their children, grieved for their dead, or dealt with life's day-by-day problems pertaining to the secular and the sacred. We have practically no information about their physical attributes or longevity. They apparently organized their lives around hunting and lived near scarce water sources. Because they were not food producers, the size of each band was probably limited to about 25 individuals. This situation may account for the great diversity observed in the styles of the stone lanceolate points.

Almost anything else said about the way of life of Florida's Paleoindians would be speculation, a path I have tried to avoid in this volume.

3

Were People in Florida
Before the Paleoindians?

In this chapter I digress somewhat from my vow not to impose my opinion when evaluating the limited evidence available for Pre-Paleoindians in Florida.

Archaeological sites at a number of locations throughout the Americas contain environmental and cultural materials purported by their excavators to be older than the universally accepted big-game-hunting Paleoindians, that is, ca. 14,000 years ago. Most of these sites have been lampooned and rejected for one or more reasons:

1. Objects are not recovered in undisturbed contexts by professional archaeologists.
2. There are no recognizable diagnostic weapons or tool styles.
3. There is no way to date the materials.
4. Sites and their contents are sparse, and no one can envisage where similar locations might occur.

It is theoretically possible that *Homo sapiens* was in the Western Hemisphere about 30,000 years ago. There are two major reasons why I do not believe people arrived much earlier. The first has to do with the evolution of modern humans and their ability to survive in harsh environments. The second has to do with crossing from the Old to the New World via the Bering Land Bridge. Geologists, climatologists, and paleobotanists have long agreed that no major obstructions existed to prohibit humans and animals from entering the North American continent prior to the onset of final glacial conditions about 25,000 years ago. This deduction is supported by research of linguists and physical anthropologists. The Yana RHS site in Siberia (Pitulko et al. 2004) has furnished concrete evidence that people were geographically poised to move east across the Bering Land Bridge 30,000 years ago. Located above the Arctic Circle about 71N, 135E, materials from this site include bone, horn, ivory, and stone artifacts as well as abundant remains of Ice Age animal species—mammoths, bison, cave lions, horses, and more.

Of course, there are other theories about how people first came to the Western Hemisphere (boat, raft, or ice floe), where they put ashore (east coast of South America, southwest coast of South America, west coast of North America, and northeast coast of North America), where they came from (northern Europe, northern Africa, southeast Asia), and when they got here (before *Homo erectus* became extinct). All of these theories await proof.

Logically, the ultimate explanation for the paucity of concrete evidence of early human presence in the Western Hemisphere is because the "trash" that survives from cultural activities of small groups 25,000–30,000 years ago is far less than that of larger populations of more recent times. To compound the situation, the world underwent vast climatic changes with the recurrence of Ice Age conditions around 22,000 years ago, culminating in the Glacial Maximum of approximately 18,000–20,000 years ago, followed by warm/cold oscillations, until modern climate finally emerged. Great rivers were born, flooded the countryside, changed courses, and eventually disappeared under mountains of sediment. Deposition and erosion buried or wiped away all traces of former landscapes. It is essential to search for remains of early immigrants to the Western Hemisphere in locations where a needed resource was available, abundant, and not subject to rapid decomposition. Barring the possibility of earthquakes or volcanic eruptions, stone quarry areas today are in the same place they were 25,000–30,000 years ago. Stone material weathers by several different mechanisms, but it seldom disappears.

During the greater part of the 1970s, I investigated the extensive chert (flint) locales of Florida and conducted excavations at three major quarry sites. Thousands of diagnostic stone implements were recovered, attesting to the fact that the quarries were heavily utilized by native peoples and were sources of a valuable raw material. Huge quantities of debitage (discarded chert) confirmed that people, then as now, waste resources when there is a surplus. The stone tools, including a Suwannee base and Paleo-indian unifacial scraper, were recovered from a sandy matrix and dated stylistically approximately 5,000–13,000 years ago. Below the sand at the Container Corporation of America site (8MR154) was a brown hardpan layer about 10–15 centimeters (4–6 inches) thick containing small, rust-colored iron concretions (Purdy 1981b).* Believing that this and older de-posits would be culturally sterile, I nevertheless used a soil auger to probe deeper. After recovering what appeared to be crude stone implements from a sandy-clay matrix below the hardpan, the decision was made to extend all excavation units to this level (Fig. 3.1).

Some of the stone specimens from the sandy clay appeared to be ex-tensively used, but no diagnostic tools were recovered, and no organic materials survived to furnish samples for radiocarbon dating (Figs. 3.2, 3.3, 3.4). C. T. Hallmark, a soils characterization specialist, determined that two lithologic discontinuities were present at the site and that they corresponded with the differences observed in the stone materials. Ther-moluminescence analysis and weathering studies independently returned dates of about 26,000–28,000 years ago on a number of samples. Because of the controversial nature of the finds and the experimental techniques used to date them, funding was not readily available to conduct much-needed additional investigations (Purdy 1981a, b, 1982–1983, 1984; Purdy and Clark 1987). The lack of continuing support to demonstrate that some stone implements can be dated by measuring patina thickness might be explained in the following way.

Since 99.9 percent of all American archaeologists (including myself) are not "scientists" by the narrow definition of that term, they were not aware of the accumulated knowledge that led to the U.S. Department of Energy funding the Materials Science Engineering Department at the University of Florida to determine the most longlasting environment in which to entomb nuclear and toxic waste. For this reason, members of

---

*The technical term for this hardpan layer is Bh horizon. It is a subsurface accumulation of humus and clay leached out of the cover sands (David Leigh, personal communication 2007).

Fig. 3.1. Barbara Purdy pointing to the area below the sand and hardpan where stone artifacts were recovered at the Container Corporation of America site (8MR154) (photo by Myles Bland).

Fig. 3.2. Artifact in place within the sandy clay at the Container Corporation of America site (8MR154).

Fig. 3.3. Examples of fairly large stone specimens exhibiting use wear from the Container Corporation of America site (8MR154).

Fig. 3.4. Examples of small stone specimens exhibiting retouch or use wear from the Container Corporation of America site (8MR154).

the department were interested in my observations about weathering at the Container site. As part of my excavations, I recovered 10,000 pieces of Florida chert from one 3-meter square. Three types of weathering were associated with stone implements that exhibited three different typologies. These included:

1. Uniform patina thickness on thousands of crude specimens from the controversial lower level at the site. These yielded the 26,000–28,000 dates based on sophisticated laboratory measurements (see 3 below).
2. Hundreds of specimens that appeared to have been manufactured using a Levallois technique came from a higher stratum and definitely had been subjected to wet/dry conditions. These specimens had no patina formation but were so weathered that nearly all of the minor elements had disappeared. These objects were not considered for the experiment.
3. Specimens that appeared virtually unweathered came from a stratum still higher in the square. Since there were diagnostic artifacts from this level, e.g., a 9,000-year-old Kirk Serrated point and the Suwannee base, they were used as a baseline for the analysis. We sacrificed the Kirk Serrated point by breaking it across the midsection and compared the slight amount of weathering after 9,000 years to the patina thickness of that on sacrificed specimens from the lower level and came up with the date of 26,000–28,000 years ago.

There is no question that weathering depends upon the environment and should not be considered either an absolute or a relative indicator of age unless the environment is known. In this case, the environment consisted of one 3-meter square. It is true that depth below surface and sediment differences might influence the analysis; on the other hand, the fact that there are sediment differences must indicate that a time factor is involved. For more about weathering, see Purdy and Clark (1987).

In the spring of 2006, with the permission and cooperation of the present landowner, William J. Whitehurst, and the help of many volunteers,

Albert C. Goodyear and I opened five deep trenches at the Container site close to the area I excavated in the 1970s. Artifacts, similar to those recovered previously, were exposed and removed from precise locations in the profile (see, for example, Fig. 3.5a, b, c). Admittedly, there are occasions when natural processes can emulate human workmanship, but there are enough examples of uniform flake removal or use wear on specimens from the sandy-clay zone at the Container site to establish that these artifacts are ancient and that they predate Paleoindian. Florida has many other ancient quarry sites, and some or all of them may contain comparable stone remains. Perhaps we need to dig deeper. Optical stimulated luminescence (OSL) may furnish a way to date the base of the sand deposit.** OSL has largely replaced the thermoluminescence method. In defense of TL analysis, however, I wonder if the method might have been perfected had it received adequate funding. The dates always fell into the ballpark of our "suspect" dates.

I was amazed to read the following paragraph in Dolan and Allen (1961: 38), which may have been taken from notes written by William Ellis Edwards and J. Clarence Simpson in the 1950s:

> A major problem in American archaeology in general and southeastern archaeology in particular is the determination of the steps in the development of the early nomadic hunters into the specialized hunter similar to the Clovis-Folsom type and the further development from the Clovis-Folsom type to the less specialized Archaic hunter and collector. The tool kit of pre-Clovis and Folsom man may be represented by unspecialized lithic implements, but, because of their generalized types, these may well have carried, accidentally or intentionally, down to historic times. The very fact that they are such generalized forms makes temporal categorization seem quite impossible.

**Investigations continue at the Container Corporation of America site. In March 2007, Dr. David Leigh, a soils morphologist at the University of Georgia, examined the profiles of a number of trenches at the site and extracted samples for OSL dating.

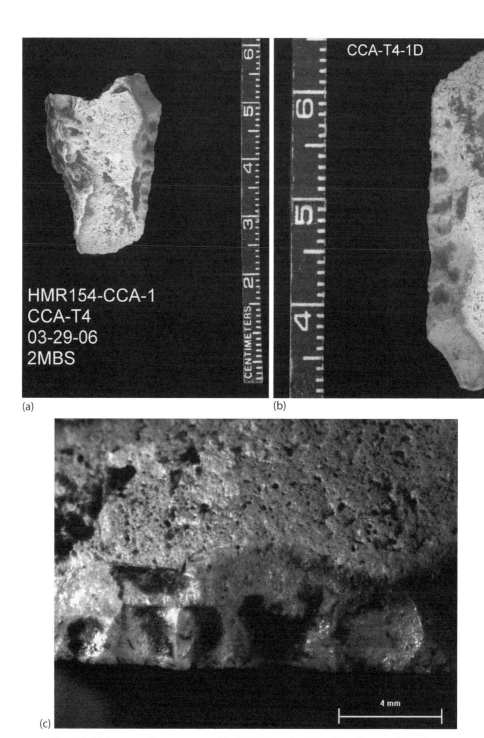

(a)

(b)

(c)

Fig. 3.5. (a) Stone artifact recovered in 2006 from the Container Corporation of America site; (b) closeup; (c) 8x magnification of used edge (courtesy of A. C. Goodyear).

I am also struck by how up to date Mason's (1962) classic article about the Paleoindian tradition is, especially the realization that we know very little more now than we did then about Pre-Paleoindians. He says:

> But assured though we may be that man had to be present in North America before those indications of his presence provided by Clovis points associated with a Late Pleistocene fauna, we are in no position to characterize that hypothetical earlier stage. None of the allegedly pre-Clovis "complexes" can be admitted with any confidence as representing what they are claimed to represent. Alleged tools of pre-Wisconsin man in America are doubly suspect at present. The geological evidence is highly debatable, and the "artifacts" are so crude as to raise the question of human authorship.
>
> This much is certain: an unknown number of men were living in large tracts of North America, and probably South America, before the last southward fluctuation of the Fourth (Wisconsin) Glaciation. For here and there, stretching back from 13,000 to 37,000 or even more years ago, are tantalizing clues that man may have been present on the American scene. This evidence is varied, vague, and indirect. (p. 121)

Container Corporation of America is the only site in Florida so far where in situ materials have been reported to date to a Pre-Paleoindian time period, although at some of the sites on the Aucilla and Wacissa rivers, a few deeply recovered organic specimens have yielded dates ranging from approximately 18,000 to 30,000 years old. They may or may not be associated with human presence.

In the final chapter, I discuss the place of quarry sites within the larger topic of Ice Age people in Florida.

4

A Rapidly Deteriorating Trail of Evidence

This chapter could easily be called "Questions Without Answers; Problems Without Solutions," and they all fall into one major category: the disappearance of critical information.

Catastrophic Events

Catastrophic events during the last few thousand years of glaciation erased, in some areas, all traces of landscapes that existed prior to about 18,000 years ago. There are no modern analogs with which to compare the rapidly changing environment that must have confronted people and animals. Rivers without water became rivers without borders within relatively brief periods of time. It is not within the scope of this volume to discuss in detail the climatic situation of the last Ice Age, but it is fascinating to imagine what it would have been like to observe the following episodes and contemplate what got swept away.

Fifteen thousand years ago, chunks of glacial ice had formed a dam above Clark Fork, Idaho, backing up a 180-mile-long lake that contained as much water as today's Erie and Ontario combined. When the dam collapsed, the water rushed westward at 45 miles per hour, creating a flood so powerful it chewed into the volcanic basalt. It followed existing drainages, created new ones, and eventually surged down the Columbia River to the Pacific Ocean carrying with it huge boulders of granite in chunks of ice it had rafted all the way from Idaho (Steury 2004).

Eighteen thousand years ago, a catastrophic flood caused by overflow and rapid lowering of Pleistocene Lake Bonneville (present-day Salt Lake) created colossal features of erosion and deposition along the Snake River. The velocity was 24 feet per second with a discharge of 14 million cubic feet per second. It scoured out basalt bedrock and rafted boulders that were more than 10 feet in diameter. The effects of the Bonneville flood can be seen for 400 miles along the Snake River as far as Hell's Canyon. Malde (1968) says that no flood recorded today comes close for velocity, discharge, or duration.

At times of maximum extent, the Laurentide ice sheet extended some 2,800 kilometers from Montana to western Pennsylvania. It began to melt about 18,000 years ago and was only 30 percent of its maximum by 12,000 years ago. When the ice began to retreat, its meltwater drained into the Gulf of Mexico via the Mississippi River, causing a major shift in isotope values. A rapid rise in sea level, apparently a surge, caused flooding of low-lying coastal areas, which must have affected people and animals living there (Brown and Kennett 1998; Kennett and Shackleton 1975).

These are only a few instances that have been documented. We need to look beneath deposits along the lower Mississippi, Columbia, Snake, Missouri, Ohio, and other large rivers. Great floods were occurring in other parts of the world at this time also and are credited with giving rise to biblical deluge stories.

Missing Records

Objects, pictures, and documents have disappeared from museum collections, making it impossible to examine them for additional facts. For instance, it would be interesting to study the stone tools from Vero (Fig. 1.8), Melbourne (Figs. 1.10, 1.12), and Helen Blazes (Figs. 1.16, 1.17), but for different reasons.

If we could see both sides of the Vero and Melbourne points (Figs. 1.8, 1.10) we could determine with more certainty that they are Paleoindian styles.

Fig. 1.12 does not look like it was made from Florida chert, and it certainly is not a Paleoindian style although reported to have come from stratum 2 at Melbourne in association with extinct fauna. This leaves us with the gnawing feeling that someone "planted" the specimen not realizing that it would do more harm than good with regard to the argument for human antiquity in the area. In the 1920s when this incident took place, no one realized that this stemmed artifact belonged to a much more recent culture. Elemental analysis could determine whether the stone is local but would not identify the culprit because all of the principals were from out of state.

Edwards (1954) described the Helen Blazes artifacts thoroughly, but they are especially valuable because of their variety and because they were recovered from stratified deposits by an anthropologist/archaeologist using anthropological and archaeological method and theory.

It is possible that many collections that seem to have gone missing are tucked away somewhere awaiting a good detective to locate them.

Another point worth mentioning is the fact that so much important information exists in unpublished reports that are not easily accessible. This situation could be equated to looters who do not notify anyone of their finds.

Uncooperative Bones

Most of the human and animal bones that have survived from the last Ice Age in Florida present a major problem. They are undatable by radiocarbon analysis because fossilization has occurred, i.e., tissues have been infiltrated by minerals turning bone into stone. Radiocarbon dating depends upon the preservation of organic carbon.

In an effort to determine if certain dense bones or teeth might retain sufficient collagen (protein) making it possible to use very small samples for accelerated mass spectroscopy (AMS C-14 dating), Dr. Thomas W. Stafford Jr. (2005) examined the Vero and Devil's Den collections of human skeletons housed in the Florida Museum of Natural History. (The animal remains from these two sites are also in the museum.) He used high resolution (70 μm) CT imaging along one to several specific planes through three fossils and total scanning on a partial maxilla of a Devil's Den individual. This work was done at Pennsylvania State DVD, Center for Quantitative Imaging. Only high resolution CT imaging is suitable for fossil analyses. Neither x-ray nor medical-resolution CT images record sufficient data. Based on these data, specific regions were selected for quantitative amino acid analysis. Amino acid analyses revealed very low to extremely low protein contents (only 0.4 to 7.4 percent of modern bone).

No dating has been attempted yet. A single tooth from the maxilla of the Devil's Den specimen could be extracted and enamel and dentine used for AMS C-14 analysis. Using twenty-first-century technology, the tooth can be reproduced by stereo lithography and replaced in the maxilla. By combining high resolution CT imaging, amino acid analyses to assess protein content, and high level chemical purification for C-14 dating, the demands of chronologists and museum scientists can be met.

Extinct Late Pleistocene animals are often associated with artifacts, but a major problem exists because it is not known if the Rancholabrean fauna are 30,000 years old or 12,000 years old. Refined methods to date faunal remains are desperately needed: new tricks with old bones!

Collectors and Construction

Locations containing human remains of great antiquity are an irreplaceable heritage, and new sites are not being created. It has been said that collectors and construction projects are an archaeologist's best friend and worst enemy. There is no question that many sites would never be found without their assistance. When I have had an opportunity to talk with amateur collectors about what archaeologists hope to learn by excavating sites in a systematic manner, they have always understood that the total information is more valuable than the isolated stone point or ceramic pot they recovered in the beginning. Unfortunately, I and other archaeologists have not been in contact with all collectors. Fairbanks's (1962) excellent article covers this topic and is recommended reading.

Construction projects are more difficult. There are a few, but not many, examples of backhoe operators stopping their machines when they notice that they have plowed through an archaeological site. The loss of critical information to private collectors and cemented landscapes is incalculable.

5

Summary and Recommendations

Since the mid-nineteenth century, enough evidence has accumulated to conclude unequivocally that humans were in Florida when many species of now-extinct animals roamed a vastly different environment in the Sunshine State. Water was scarce, forcing people and beasts to congregate around rivers, springs, sinks, and nearby terrestrial sites where thousands of lanceolate points, other implements of stone, and dozens of ivory and bone tools have been recovered. Many of these locations are described in this book.

But the story is not complete. Frustrating unsolved problems persist primarily because methods of dating fossilized bone have not been developed. At Vero and Melbourne, for instance, the presence of all animals but human was not questioned as being part of the Late Pleistocene bone bed. Since 1916, this association is still controversial, and it is still not known if this Rancholabrean fauna is 30,000 years old or 12,000 years old. Research needs to be conducted to determine if inorganic components of bone (i.e., bone apatite) might be datable (Thomas W. Stafford Jr., personal communication, 2005).

For generations, people have wondered what caused the extinction of the Late Pleistocene megafauna. Was it a catastrophic event or did it occur gradually? Epidemics, overhunting, and disrupted habitat owing to rapid climatic changes are theories that have been advanced to explain their quite sudden demise. But we really do not know, and will not know, unless we can date the bones.

Other unanswered questions pertain not only to Florida but also to the time of the arrival of people in the Western Hemisphere. Why do

Clovis sites and artifacts appear so suddenly throughout North America with virtually no apparent antecedents? The answer may be found in what C. Vance Haynes Jr. has termed the Clovis drought (Haynes 1991). When small hunting and gathering bands were spread out over the continent prior to Clovis, the "trash" they left behind would not endure in quantities large enough to be recognized. If freshwater became scarce or disappeared, then populations of humans and animals would congregate around areas such as springs where this essential resource was still available. This situation appears to explain the abrupt visibility of Clovis.

Pre-Clovis, if it does exist, probably began around 25,000–30,000 years ago and not just prior to 14,000 years ago. Since populations would have remained small throughout this entire span of time, it is understandable that sites have not been found with convincing quantities of humans, animals, or artifacts, especially when most of these items are composed of organic materials that deteriorate rapidly. Even Clovis remains are scant when compared with ceramic period cultures, illustrating that detritus increases exponentially as populations grow. For this reason, it is important to turn attention to areas, such as quarry sites, where a needed resource survives in abundance. Research projects at quarry sites throughout the Americas, if designed properly, may furnish unquestionable information to prove or refute the presence of people in the Western Hemisphere 25,000–30,000 years ago.

Is it a coincidence that beveled ivory points from Florida are identical to those of the Upper Paleolithic 30,000 years ago in the Old World? This was an age of cultural fluorescence that began shortly after modern humans appear to have replaced Neanderthals and became the only remaining species of *Homo sapiens*. This period is quite thoroughly documented and includes cultures in Central and Eastern Europe known as Perigordian and Aurignacian with well-developed bone technology. This technology and those who invented it entered the Americas and dispersed. There is genetic evidence suggesting that there were several human migrations into the Americas, some more ancient than others. The ultimate answer to the time of human entry into the Western Hemisphere, and from where, may come from new research being conducted with genetic relationships, but this will be possible only if descendants of the earliest inhabitants have survived.

It is hoped that an energetic researcher will attack the problems mentioned and *prove* beyond speculation that this hemisphere was inhabited earlier than existing factual evidence suggests.

Bibliography

Adair, James. 1775. *The History of the American Indians*. Printed for Edward and Charles Dilly, London. A later printing in 1930 was edited by Samuel Cole Williams, LLD, and published by Promontory Press, New York.

Agassiz, Jean Louis Rodolphe. 1854. William Usher's chapter on Geology and Paleontology, pp. 352–353. In *Types of Mankind*, Vol. 4, edited by Josiah C. Nott and George R. Gliddon. Lippincott, Grambo & Co., Philadelphia.

Andrews, Terri J. 2006. Native American Stories of Creation. *A Good Red Road* (a bimonthly Native American newsletter).

Arnold, J. R., and W. F. Libby. 1949. Age Determinations by Radiocarbon Content, Checks with Samples of Known Age. *Science* 110: 678–680.

Berry, Edward W. 1917. The Fossil Plants from Vero, Florida. *Florida State Geological Survey*, 9th Annual Report, pp. 19–33.

Brown, P. A., and J. P. Kennett. 1998. Megaflood Erosion and Meltwater Plumbing Changes During Last North American Deglaciation in the Gulf of Mexico Sediments. *Geology* 26(7): 599–602.

Bullen, Ripley P. 1949. The Woodward Site. *The Florida Anthropologist* 2(3–4): 49–64.

———. 1958. *The Bolen Bluff Site on Paynes Prairie, Florida*. Contributions of the Florida State Museum, Social Sciences No. 4.

———. 1968. *A Guide to the Identification of Florida Projectile Points*. Florida State Museum, Gainesville.

———. 1969. A Clovis Fluted Point from the Santa Fe River. *The Florida Anthropologist* 22(1–4): 36–37.

———. 1975. *A Guide to the Identification of Florida Projectile Points*. Revised edition. Kendall Books, Gainesville.

Bullen, Ripley P., and Edward M. Dolan. 1959. The Johnson Lake Site, Marion County, Florida. *The Florida Anthropologist* 12(4): 77–94.

Bullen, Ripley P., S. David Webb, and Benjamin I. Waller. 1970. A Worked Mammoth Bone from Florida. *American Antiquity* 35(2): 203–205.

Clausen, Carl Jon. 1964. The A-356 Site and the Florida Archaic. M.A. thesis, Department of Anthropology, University of Florida.

Clausen, Carl J., H. K. Brooks, and Al B. Wesolowsky. 1975a. The Early Man Site at Warm Mineral Springs, Florida. *Journal of Field Archaeology* 2(3): 191–213.

———. 1975b. Florida Spring Confirmed as 10,000 Year Old Early Man Site. *The Florida Anthropologist* 28 (Part 2): 1–38.

Clausen, C. J., A. D. Cohen, Cesare Emiliani, J. A. Holman, and J. J. Stipp. 1979. Little Salt Spring, Florida: A Unique Underwater Site. *Science* 203(4381): 609–614.

Cockrell, W. A., and Larry Murphy. 1978. Pleistocene Man in Florida. *Archaeology of Eastern North America* 6: 1–13.

Converse, Howard H., Jr. 1973. *A Pleistocene Vertebrate Fauna from Palm Beach County, Florida.* Plaster Jacket 21, Florida State Museum, Gainesville.

Cooke, Wythe. 1926. Fossil Man and Pleistocene Vertebrates in Florida. *American Journal of Science* 12: 441–452.

Cooke, C. Wythe, and Stuart Mossom. 1929. Geology of Florida. *Florida Geological Survey*, 20th Annual Report, pp. 29–227.

Daniel, I. R., and M. Wisenbaker. 1987. *Harney Flats: A Florida Paleo-Indian Site.* Baywood Publishing Company, Inc., Farmingdale, N.Y.

Dixon, E. James. 1999. *Bones, Boats, & Bison.* University of New Mexico Press, Albuquerque.

Dolan, Edward M., and Glenn T. Allen, Jr. 1961. An Investigation of the Darby and Hornsby Springs Sites, Alachua County, Florida. *Florida Geological Survey Special Publications* 7: 1–124.

Dunbar, James S. 1991. Resource Orientation of Clovis and Suwannee Age Paleoindian Sites in Florida. In *Clovis Origins and Adaptations*, edited by Robson Bonnichsen and Karen Turnmire, pp. 185–213. Center for the Study of the First Americans, Corvallis, Oregon.

———. 1996. Enigmatic Bola Date Resolved. *Aucilla River Times* 9(1): 10.

———. 2002. Chronostratigraphy and Paleoclimate of Late Pleistocene Florida and the Implications of Changing Land Use. M.S. thesis, Department of Anthropology, Florida State University, Tallahassee.

Dunbar, James S., and C. Andrew Hemmings. 2004. Paleoindian Points and Knives. In *New Perspectives on the First Americans*, edited by Bradley T. Lepper and Robson Bonnichsen, pp. 65–72. Texas A&M University Press, College Station.

Dunbar, James S., and Ben I. Waller. 1983. A Distribution Analysis of the Clovis/Suwannee Paleo-Indian Sites of Florida—A Geographic Approach. *Florida Anthropologist* 36(1–2): 40–66.

Dunbar, James S., and S. David Webb. 1996. Bone and Ivory Tools from Submerged Paleoindian Sites in Florida. In *The Paleoindian and Early Archaic Southeast*, edited by D. G. Anderson and K. E. Sassaman, pp. 331–352. University of Alabama Press. Tuscaloosa.

Edwards, William Ellis. 1954. The Helen Blazes Site of Central-Eastern Florida: A Study of Method Utilizing the Disciplines of Archeology, Geology, and Pedology. Submitted in partial fulfillment of the requirements for the degree of Doctor of Philosophy, Faculty of Political Science, Columbia University.

Fagan, Brian M. 1991. *In the Beginning: An Introduction to Archaeology.* 7th edition. HarperCollins, New York.

Fairbanks, Charles H. 1962. The Contribution of the Amateur. *The Florida Anthropologist* 15(1): 13–20.

Farr, Grayal E. 2006. A Reevaluation of Bullen's Typology for Preceramic Projectile Points. Master's thesis, Department of Anthropology, Florida State University, Tallahassee.

Faught, Michael K. 1999. PaleoAucilla Prehistory—Clovis Underwater '98. *Aucilla River Times* 7(1): 5.

Gidley, James W. 1927. Investigating Evidence of Early Man in Florida. Smithsonian Institution, Explorations and Field Work in 1926, *Smithsonian Miscellaneous Collections* 78(7): 168–174.

———. 1929. Ancient Man in Florida: Further Investigations. *Bulletin of the Geological Society of America* 40: 491–502.

———. 1930. Investigations of Early Man in Florida. Smithsonian Institution Exploration and Field Work in 1929, *Smithsonian Miscellaneous Collections* 81: 37–38.

Gidley, James W., and Frederic B. Loomis. 1926. Fossil Man in Florida. *American Journal of Science* 12 (September): 254–264.

Gifford, John A. 2006. Little Salt Spring: Overview. Symposium on Little Salt Spring, June 11, 2006, Northport, Florida.

Goggin, John M. 1950. An Early Lithic Complex from Central Florida. *American Antiquity* 16(1): 46–49.

———. 1960. Underwater Archaeology: Its Nature and Limitations. *American Antiquity* 25(3): 348–354.

———. 1962. Recent Developments in Underwater Archaeology. Proceedings of the 16th Southeastern Archaeological Conference. *Southeastern Archaeological Conference Newsletter* 8: 77–88.

Gomez, Rick, and Casey Coy. 2006. Exploring the Depths of Little Salt Spring. Symposium on Little Salt Spring, June 11, 2006, Northport, Florida.

Goodyear, Albert C., Sam B. Upchurch, Mark J. Brooks, and Nancy N. Goodyear. 1983. Paleo-Indian Manifestations in the Tampa Bay Region, Florida. *The Florida Anthropologist* 36(1–2): 40–66.

Haynes, C. Vance, Jr. 1991. Geoarchaeological and Paleohydrological Evidence for a Clovis-Age Drought in North America and Its Bearing on Extinction. *Quarternary Research* 35: 438–450.

Heilprin, Angelo. 1887. Explorations on the West Coast of Florida, and in the Okechobee Wilderness. *Transactions of the Wagner Free Institute of Science*, vol. 1. Philadelphia.

Hemmings, Christopher Andrew. 2004. The Organic Clovis: A Single Continent-Wide Cultural Adaptation. Ph.D. dissertation, Department of Anthropology, University of Florida.

Hemmings, E. Thomas. 1975. The Silver Springs Site, Prehistory in the Silver Springs Valley, Florida. *The Florida Anthropologist* 28(4): 141–158.

Hoffman, Charles A. 1983. A Mammoth Kill Site in the Silver Springs Run. *The Florida Anthropologist* 36(1–2): 83–87.

Holman, Alan J., and Carl J. Clausen. 1984. Fossil Vertebrates Associated with Paleo-Indian Artifacts at Little Salt Spring, Florida. *Journal of Vertebrate Paleontology* 4(1): 146–154.

Holmes, W. H. 1919. Handbook of Aboriginal American Antiquities, Part I: Introductory: The Lithic Industries. *Bureau of American Ethnology Bulletin* 60. Washington, D.C.

Hrdlička, Aleš. 1907. Skeletal Remains Suggesting or Attributed to Early Man in North America. *Bureau of American Ethnology Bulletin* 33. Washington, D.C.

———. 1918. Recent Discoveries Attributed to Early Man in America. *Bureau of American Ethnology Bulletin* 66. Washington, D.C.

Hulbert, Richard C., Jr. 2001. *The Fossil Vertebrates of Florida*. University Press of Florida, Gainesville.

Jenks, Albert Ernest, and Mrs. H. H. Simpson, Sr. 1941. Beveled Artifacts in Florida of the Same Type as Artifacts Found near Clovis, New Mexico. *American Antiquity* 6(4): 314–319.

Jennings, Jesse D. 1974. Across an Arctic Bridge. In *The World of the American Indian*, edited by Jules B. Billard, pp. 29–69. National Geographic Society, Washington, D.C.

Kennett, James P., and N. J. Shackleton. 1975. Laurentide Ice Sheet Meltwater Recorded in Gulf of Mexico Deep-Sea Cores. *Science* 188 (April 11): 147–150.

King, James. 1975. Analysis of Pollen from Warm Mineral Springs, Unpublished manuscript on file, Underwater Archaeological Research, Department of State, Tallahassee.

Koski, Steve. 2006. Recent Research at Little Salt Spring. Symposium on Little Salt Spring, June 11, 2006, Northport, Florida.

Leidy, Joseph. 1889. Notice of Some Fossil Human Bones. *Transactions of the Wagner Free Institute of Science* 2. Philadelphia.

Loomis, Frederic B. 1924. Artifacts Associated with the Remains of a Columbian Elephant at Melbourne, Florida. *American Journal of Science* 8(48): 503–508.

Lyell, Sir Charles. 1863. *The Geological Evidences of the Antiquity of Man*. John Murray, London.

MacCurdy, George Grant, ed. 1937. *Early Man*. Books for Libraries Press, Freeport, New York.

Malde, Harold E. 1968. *The Catastrophic Late Pleistocene Bonneville Flood in the Snake River Plain, Idaho*. Geological Survey Professional Paper 596. U.S. Geological Survey, Washington.

Martin, Richard A. 1966. *Eternal Spring*. Great Outdoors Publishing Co., St. Petersburg, Florida.

Martin, Robert A., and S. David Webb. 1974. Late Pleistocene Mammals from the Devil's Den Fauna, Levy County, Florida. In *Pleistocene Mammals of Florida*, edited by S. David Webb. University of Florida Press, Gainesville.

Martini, I., M. Brookfield, and S. Sadura. 2001. *Principles of Glacial Geomorphology and Geology: Upper Saddle River*. Prentice-Hall, New York.

Mason, Ronald J. 1962. The Paleo-Indian Tradition in Eastern North America. *Current Anthropology* 3(3): 227–283.

McDonald, H. Gregory. 1975. The Warm Mineral Springs Fauna. Unpublished manuscript on file, Underwater Archaeological Research, Department of State, Tallahassee.

Merriam, John C. 1914. Preliminary Report on the Discovery of Human Remains in an Asphalt Deposit at Rancho La Brea. *Science* 40: 198–203.

———. 1935. Review of Evidence Relating to the Status of the Problem of Antiquity of Man in Florida. *Science* 82(2118): 103.

Morris, Donald H. 1975. Warm Mineral Springs Man. Unpublished manuscript on file, Division of Historical Research, Department of State, Tallahassee.

Neill, Wilfred T. 1958. A Stratified Early Site at Silver Springs, Florida. *The Florida Anthropologist* 11: 33–52.

———. 1964. The Association of Suwannee Points and Extinct Animals in Florida. *The Florida Anthropologist* 17: 17–32.

———. A Florida Paleo-Indian Implement. 1971. *The Florida Anthropologist* 24(2): 61–70.

Nott, Josiah C., and George R. Gliddon, eds. 1854. *Types of Mankind*, 8th edition. Lippincott, Grambo & Co., Philadelphia.

Olsen, Stanley J. 1958. The Wakulla Cave. *Natural History* 67(7): 396–398, 401–403.

Pitulko, V. V., et al. Yana RHS Site: Humans in the Arctic Before the Last Glacial Maximum. *Science* 303 (5654): 52–56.

Purdy, Barbara A. 1975. The Senator Edwards Chipped Stone Workshop Site (8–Mr-122), Marion County, Florida: A Preliminary Report of Investigations. *The Florida Anthropologist* 28: 178–189.

———. 1981a. *Florida's Prehistoric Stone Technology*. University Press of Florida. Gainesville.

———. 1981b. Investigations into the Use of Chert Outcrops by Prehistoric Floridians: The Container Corporation of America Site. *The Florida Anthropologist* 34(2): 90–108.

———. 1982–1983. Early Man Research in Southeastern North America: New Developments. *Early Man News* 7/8, pp. 19–29. Edited for the Commission for the Paleoecology of Early Man of INQUA (International Union for Quaternary Research), Tübingen.

———. 1984. Quarry Studies: Technological and Chronological Significance. In *Prehistoric Quarries and Lithic Production*, edited by Jonathon E. Ericson and Barbara A. Purdy, pp. 119–127. Cambridge University Press, London.

———. 1991 *The Art and Archaeology of Florida's Wetlands*. CRC Press, Boca Raton.

———. 1996. *How to Do Archaeology: The Right Way*. University Press of Florida, Gainesville.

———. 2001. Archaeological Investigations of Water-Saturated Deposits in Volusia County, Florida: Groves Orange Midden on Lake Monroe. In *Enduring Records: The Environmental and Cultural Heritage of Wetlands*, edited by Barbara A. Purdy. Oxbow Books, Oxford, England.

Purdy, Barbara A., and David E. Clark. 1987. Weathering of Inorganic Materials: Dating and Other Applications. In *Advances in Archaeological Method and Theory*, Volume 11, edited by Michael B. Schiffer. Academic Press, Inc., New York.

Rachels, Thomas, and Robert L. Knight. 2004. Dimple Stones: An Unique and Early

Ground Stone Artifact Type from the Southeast. *The Amateur Archaeologist* 10(2): 57–76.

Randazzo, A. F., and D. S. Jones, eds. 1997 *The Geology of Florida*. University Press of Florida, Gainesville.

Rayl, Sandra L. 1974. A Paleo-Indian Mammoth Kill Site Near Silver Springs, Florida. Master's thesis on file, Department of Anthropology, Northern Arizona University.

Renfrew, Colin, and Paul Bahn. 1991. *Archaeology: Theories, Methods, and Practice*. Thames and Hudson, New York.

Roberts, Frank H. H. 1937. The Folsom Problem in North American Archaeology. In *Early Man*, edited by George Grant MacCurdy, pp. 153–162. Books for Libraries Press, Freeport, New York.

Rosenau, J. C., G. L. Faulkner, C. W. Hendry, Jr., and R. W. Hull. 1977. *Springs of Florida*. Florida Geological Survey Bulletin 31, revised. Tallahassee.

Rouse, Irving. 1951. *A Survey of Indian River Archeology, Florida*. Yale University Publications in Anthropology No. 44. Yale University Press, New Haven.

Royal, William R., with Robert F. Burgess. 1978. *The Man Who Rode Sharks*. Dodd, Mead, & Company, New York.

Royal, William R., and Eugenie Clark. 1960. Natural Preservation of Human Brain, Warm Mineral Springs, Florida. *American Antiquity* 26(2): 285–287.

Ruppé, Reynold J. 1980. *The Archaeology of Drowned Terrestrial Sites: Underwater Archaeological Research at the Venice Site*. In Bureau of Historic Sites and Properties, Bulletin No. 6, pp. 33–80. (With contributions by other authors.)

Scott, Thomas M., Guy H. Means, Rebecca P. Meegan, Ryan C. Means, Sam B. Upchurch, R. E. Copeland, James Jones, Tina Roberts, and Alan Willet. 2004. *Springs of Florida*. Florida Geological Survey, Bulletin No. 66. Tallahassee.

Sellards, E. H. 1912. The Soils and Other Surface Residual Materials of Florida. *Florida Geological Survey*, 4th Annual Report, p. 18. Tallahassee.

———. 1916a. Human Remains and Associated Fossils from the Pleistocene of Florida. *Florida Geological Survey*, 8th Annual Report, pp. 123–160. Tallahassee.

———. 1916b. Human Remains from the Pleistocene of Florida. *Science*, n.s. 44(1139): 615–617.

———. 1916c. Fossil Vertebrates from Florida: A New Miocene Fauna; New Pliocene Species; the Pleistocene Fauna. *Florida Geological Survey*, 8th Annual Report, pp. 77–120.

———. 1940. Early Man in America, Index to Localities and Selected Bibliography. *Geological Society of America [Bulletin]* 51: 373–431.

Sellards, E. H., Rollin T. Chamberlin, T. Wayland Vaughan, A. Hrdlička, O. P. Hay, and G. G. MacCurdy. 1917. Symposium on the Age and Relations of the Fossil Human Remains Found at Vero, Florida. *Journal of Geology* 25: 1–62.

Shackleton, Nicholas J., and Neil D. Opdyke. 1973. Oxygen Isotope and Palaeomagnetic Stratigraphy of Equatorial Pacific Core V28–238; Oxygen Isotope Temperatures and Ice Volumes on a 105 Year and 106 Year Scale. *Quaternary Research* 3(1): 39–55.

Sheldon, Elizabeth, and Marguerita I. Cameron. 1976. Reconstruction of Prehistoric Environments: The Warm Mineral Springs Project. *Southeastern Archaeological Conference Bulletin* 19: 68–69.

Simpson, George Gaylord. 1930. *Additions to the Pleistocene of Florida*. American Museum Novitates No. 406. The American Museum of Natural History, New York.

Simpson, J. Clarence. 1948. Folsom-Like Points from Florida. *The Florida Anthropologist* 1(1–2): 11–15.

Skow, John. 1986. This Florida Spa Holds a Surprising Lode of Prehistory. *Smithsonian* 17(9): 73–83.

Stafford, Thomas W., Jr. 2005. Fossil Human Remains from Sites in Florida. Containing Extinct Late Pleistocene Megafauna: Assessing 14C Dating Feasibility by Using High Resolution CT Scanning and Geochemical Analyses. Poster prepared for Clovis in the Southeast Conference, Columbia, South Carolina, October 26–29.

Steury, Tim. 2004. An Exquisite Scar. [About the Channeled Scablands]. *Washington State University Magazine*, Fall: 38–43.

Stewart, T. Dale. 1946. A Reexamination of the Fossil Human Skeletal Remains from Melbourne, Florida with Further Data on the Vero Skull. *Smithsonian Miscellaneous Collections*, vol. 106, no. 10.

Swanton, John R. 1946. *The Indians of the Southeastern United States*. Smithsonian Institution Press, Washington, D.C.

Tesar, Louis D. 1994. Clubheads, Bola Stones, or What? *The Florida Anthropologist* 47(3): 295–303.

Tesar, Louis D., and B. Calvin Jones. 2000. Wakulla Springs Lodge Site (2WA329): A Preliminary Report on a Stratified Paleoindian Through Archaic Site, Wakulla County, Florida. *The Florida Anthropologist* 53(2–3): 98–114.

———. 2004. Wakulla Springs Lodge Site (2WA329) in Edward Ball Wakulla Springs State Park, Wakulla County, Florida: A Summary of Eleven Projects and Management Recommendations. Bureau of Archaeological Research, Division of Historical Resources, Florida Department of State, Tallahassee.

Townshend, F. Trench. 1875. *Wild Life in Florida*. Hurst & Blackett, London.

Vaughan, T. W. 1907. Report on the Localities at Which Were Found the Fossil Human Remains on Sarasota Bay. *Bureau of American Ethnology Bulletin* 33: 64–66. Washington.

Waller, Ben I. 1969. Paleo-Indian and Other Artifacts from a Florida Stream Bed. *The Florida Anthropologist* 22: 37–39.

———. 1970. Some Occurences of Paleo-Indian Projectile Points in Florida Waters. *The Florida Anthropologist* 23: 129–134.

———. 1983. Florida Anthropologist Interview with Ben Waller. *The Florida Anthropologist* 36(1–2): 31–39. (Interview conducted by James Dunbar.)

Waller, Ben I., and James Dunbar. 1977. Distribution of Paleo-Indian Projectiles in Florida. *The Florida Anthropologist* 30(2): 79–80.

Warren, Lyman O. 1966. A Possible Paleo-Indian Site in Pinellas County. *The Florida Anthroologist* 24: 39–41.

———. 1968. Caladesi Causeway: A Possible Inundated Paleo-Indian Workshop. *The Florida Anthropologist* 21: 92–94.

Webb, S. David, ed. 1974. *Pleistocene Mammals of Florida*. University of Florida Press, Gainesville.

———. 2006. *First Floridians and Last Mastodons: The Page-Ladson Site on the Aucilla River*. Springer, The Netherlands.

Webb, S. David, and C. Andrew Hemmings. 2001. Ivory and Bone Tools from Late Pleistocene Deposits in the Aucilla and Wacissa Rivers, North-Central Florida. In *Enduring Records: The Environmental and Cultural Heritage of Wetlands*, edited by Barbara A. Purdy, pp. 1–8. Oxbow Books, Oxford, England.

Webb, S. David, James S. Dunbar, and Benjamin I. Waller. 1990. Ecological Implications of Ivory Foreshafts from Underwater Sites in Florida. Paper presented at the International Council for Archaeozoology, Sixth International Conference, May 21–25, Smithsonian Institution, Washington, D.C.

Webb, S. David, Jerald T. Milanich, Roger Alexson, and James Dunbar. 1983. An Extinct *Bison* Kill Site, Jefferson County, Florida. *The Florida Anthropologist* 36(1–2): 81–82.

———. 1984. A *Bison antiquus* Kill Site, Wacissa River, Jefferson County, Florida. *American Antiquity* 49(2): 384–392.

Weigel, Robert D. 1963. Fossil Vertebrates of Vero, Florida. *Florida Geological Survey*, Special Publication No. 10. Tallahassee.

Wyman, Jeffries. 1875. Fresh-Water Shell Mounds of the St. John's River, Florida. *Peabody Academy of Science*, Salem, Massachusetts.

Zarikian, Carlos A. Alvarez, Peter K. Swart, John A. Gifford, and Patricia L. Blackwelder. 2005. Holocene Paleohydrology of Little Salt Spring, Florida, Based on Ostracod Assemblages and Stable Isotopes. *Palaeogeography, Palaeoclimatology, Palaeoecology* 225(2005): 134–156.

Index

Barbara A. Purdy is professor emerita of anthropology at the University of Florida. She is also curator emerita in archaeology at the Florida Museum of Natural History.

Related-interest titles from University Press of Florida

Archeology of the Florida Gulf Coast
Gordon R. Willey

The Archaeology and History of the Native Georgia Tribes
Max E. White

Braindance: New Discoveries about Human Origins and Brain Evolution,
Revised and Expanded Edition
Dean Falk

The Calusa and Their Legacy: South Florida People and Their Environments
Darcie A. MacMahon and William H. Marquardt

Florida's Indians from Ancient Times to the Present
Jerald T. Milanich

Fossiling in Florida: A Guide for Diggers and Divers
Mark Renz

How to Do Archaeology the Right Way
Barbara A. Purdy

Indian Art of Ancient Florida
Barbara A. Purdy

For more information on these and other books, visit our Web site at www.upf.com.